The convergence of narrative in film, video gam[e]
mentally change the entertainment industry in coming years. Chris Solarski's book gives content creators essential insights into interactive story composition and how to adapt these concepts for transmedia storytelling.

Marc Forster
Film Director and *Producer*

The clever thing about this book is that it bridges the worlds of game design and storytelling. I would recommend this to anyone who wants to get into game design and understand what's going on beneath the surface. It reminds me of Robert McKee's *Story*, the classic book on screenwriting. You read it and you think: Aha, this is how storytelling works in film, it really can be explained! And you can see this book as a companion volume that is essentially doing the same thing for games.

Tom Standage
Deputy Editor and *Digital Strategist*
of The Economist and New York Times *Bestselling Author*

As a gamification designer you look for inspiration from multiple sources to create behavior change and evoke emotions that help your audience make decisions. Chris Solarski brilliantly captures how dynamic composition techniques for transmedia storytelling can assist in reaching your audience through shapes, flow, positioning, and much more.

An Coppens
Chief Game Changer at Gamification Nation Ltd.

INTERACTIVE STORIES AND
VIDEO GAME ART

A STORYTELLING FRAMEWORK
FOR GAME DESIGN

INTERACTIVE STORIES AND
VIDEO GAME ART

A STORYTELLING FRAMEWORK FOR GAME DESIGN

Chris Solarski

CRC Press
Taylor & Francis Group
Boca Raton London New York

CRC Press is an imprint of the
Taylor & Francis Group, an **informa** business

AN A K PETERS BOOK

Cover portrait photo: Erica Swearingen, Photographer (agameartist@hotmail.com)

CRC Press
Taylor & Francis Group
6000 Broken Sound Parkway NW, Suite 300
Boca Raton, FL 33487-2742

© 2017 by Chris Solarski
CRC Press is an imprint of Taylor & Francis Group, an Informa business

No claim to original U.S. Government works

Printed on acid-free paper
Version Date: 20160922

International Standard Book Number-13: 978-1-4987-8150-3 (Paperback)

This book contains information obtained from authentic and highly regarded sources. While all reasonable efforts have been made to publish reliable data and information, neither the author[s] nor the publisher can accept any legal responsibility or liability for any errors or omissions that may be made. The publishers wish to make clear that any views or opinions expressed in this book by individual editors, authors or contributors are personal to them and do not necessarily reflect the views/opinions of the publishers. The information or guidance contained in this book is intended for use by medical, scientific or health-care professionals and is provided strictly as a supplement to the medical or other professional's own judgement, their knowledge of the patient's medical history, relevant manufacturer's instructions and the appropriate best practice guidelines. Because of the rapid advances in medical science, any information or advice on dosages, procedures or diagnoses should be independently verified. The reader is strongly urged to consult the relevant national drug formulary and the drug companies' and device or material manufacturers' printed instructions, and their websites, before administering or utilizing any of the drugs, devices or materials mentioned in this book. This book does not indicate whether a particular treatment is appropriate or suitable for a particular individual. Ultimately it is the sole responsibility of the medical professional to make his or her own professional judgements, so as to advise and treat patients appropriately. The authors and publishers have also attempted to trace the copyright holders of all material reproduced in this publication and apologize to copyright holders if permission to publish in this form has not been obtained. If any copyright material has not been acknowledged please write and let us know so we may rectify in any future reprint.

Except as permitted under U.S. Copyright Law, no part of this book may be reprinted, reproduced, transmitted, or utilized in any form by any electronic, mechanical, or other means, now known or hereafter invented, including photocopying, microfilming, and recording, or in any information storage or retrieval system, without written permission from the publishers.

For permission to photocopy or use material electronically from this work, please access www.copyright.com (http://www.copyright.com/) or contact the Copyright Clearance Center, Inc. (CCC), 222 Rosewood Drive, Danvers, MA 01923, 978-750-8400. CCC is a not-for-profit organization that provides licenses and registration for a variety of users. For organizations that have been granted a photocopy license by the CCC, a separate system of payment has been arranged.

Trademark Notice: Product or corporate names may be trademarks or registered trademarks, and are used only for identification and explanation without intent to infringe.

Library of Congress Cataloging-in-Publication Data

Library of Congress Cataloging-in-Publication Data
Name: Solarski, Chris, author.
Title: Interactive stories and video game art : a storytelling framework for game design / Chris Solarski.
Description: Boca Raton, FL : Taylor & Francis, 2016.
Identifiers: LCCN 2016022988 | ISBN 9781498781503 (pbk. : alk. paper)
Subjects: LCSH: Video games--Authorship. | Video games--Design. | Storytelling.
Classification: LCC GV1469.34.A97 S65 2016 | DDC 794.8/1536--dc23
LC record available at https://lccn.loc.gov/2016022988

Visit the Taylor & Francis Web site at
http://www.taylorandfrancis.com

and the CRC Press Web site at
http://www.crcpress.com

For my two joys,
Chickpea and Charlie.

Contents

Section I   Primary Shapes and Dynamic Composition

Section II   The Dramatic Curve and Transitions

Preface

My first book, *Drawing Basics and Video Game Art: Classic to Cutting-Edge Art Techniques for Winning Video Game Design* (*DBaVGA*) (Watson-Guptill), was published in 2012. As of 2016, *DBaVGA* has been translated into Japanese and Korean, and is used by developers, students, and teachers of game art around the world. The book's success is far greater than I'd ever imagined! And yet, I feel that *DBaVGA*'s focus on game art means that there's a missed opportunity for a broader audience to benefit from the wealth of fundamental design principles inspired by classical art.

My lifelong commitment to research and personal development is especially important to me, and since 2012, I have been investigating the intersections between film storytelling techniques and interactive art to help me better understand the mechanisms involved in conveying emotionally complex narrative experiences in video games. It is through this continued research that I realized the topic of this book, *Interactive Stories and Video Game Art: A Storytelling Framework for Game Design*, and a way to adapt the concepts presented in *DBaVGA* to the concerns of the whole development team. I was further motivated to write *Interactive Stories and Video Game Art* because the existing books on storytelling in games approach the topic from a scriptwriter's perspective while the player's experience is primarily conveyed through interaction, visuals, and audio. This book is therefore my attempt to define the unique and powerful art of storytelling in video games through the strengths that are fundamental to the art form. I hope you will find the techniques contained in the following pages insightful and inspiring for all your video game and interactive art projects.

I am eternally grateful to the Swiss Arts Council, Pro Helvetia, for its ongoing support of my work. It is thanks to my involvement in the organization's Game Culture Initiative (2010–2012) that sparked my continued fascination in the overlap between traditional art, film, and video games.

#SwissGames

Acknowledgments

I could not have written this book without the combined encouragement, critical feedback, and support from the many generous people and organizations that have inspired me and pushed my work forward during the past 15, or so, years. There are many people to thank! I therefore wish to apologize in advance if I have accidentally excluded anybody from the following list who should rightfully be mentioned. My deepest gratitude goes to (in alphabetical order).

The following organizations:
AlpICT, Born Digital, Inc., the Embassy of Switzerland in Japan, EPAC Academy of Contemporary Arts, International Game Developers Association, IGDA Japan, NASSCOM, Pro Helvetia, Pro Helvetia New Delhi, SAE Zurich, SAE Geneva, the Swiss Game Developers Association, and swissnex.

The following individuals:
Adel Rosario, Aïda Suljicic, Alastair Ingason, Alex Pons Carden-Jones, Alice Lee, Amanda Mills, Amparo Meier, Andi Bissig and Michel Barengo at Pocket Universe Productions, Andreas Rufer, Anita Martinecz, Anne-Christine Gascoigne, Antoine Delacrétaz, Amit Goyal and Arjun Gopalin at SuperSike Games, Dr. Balz Strasser, Dr. Bob Sumner, Björn Schmelter, Brendan Kelly, Chandrika Grover Ralleigh, Chino Noris, Christian Nutt, Christian Wittmer, Christine Matthey, Claudia and Matteo Molinari at We Are Müesli, Clifford Phillips, Daniel Frei, Damyan Kristof, Danilo "DJ" Walde, Dave Pharo, David Canella (*MODSORK*), Dominik Marosi, Don Schmocker, Dorian Iten, Doug Lipman at Story Dynamics, Dragica Kahlina, Elias Farhan, Erica Swearingen, Erik Fonseka, Eugeninya Kareva, Gabriel Gomes Fidalgo, Georg Bleikolm, Guillaume de Fondaumière, Gustavo Sánchez Pérez, Iain McCaig, Inn-Yang Low, Janina Woods, Jamie Mooney, Jasmin Widmer and Yasemin Günay and the Koboldgames team, Jean Snow, Jenova Chen, Jessica Vega, Johann Recordon,

John Willimann, Johnny Linnert, Kaspar Manz, Kath Bartholomew, Kenji Ono, Lalima Singh, Linda Leggio, Luc Meier, Luca Cannellotto, Luca Giarrizzo, Luci Holland, Luke Newell, Madlaina Kalunder, Makiko Ohira, Małgosia Hirayama, Manav Sachdev, Marc Bodmer, Marc Schärer at dreamora, Marco Plüss, Maria Woodliff, Markus Jost, Martha Moran, Martina Hugentobler, Matt Nava, Matt Rusiniak, Meredith Fields, Michael Mentler, Michael Rob, Michel Vust, Miguel Perez-La Plante, Mike Lewin, Miyuki Ogata, Nicolas Galan, Nina Kiel, Nick Ghangass, Nils Ammann, Olga Novosselova, Oliver Miescher, Paolo Branca, Patrizia Adberhalden, Paul Hellard, Paul Toprac, Patrick Barb, Pascal Mueller, Phil Hale, Phil McCammon, Philippe Kopajtic, Philomena Schwab, Rahel Kamber, Rai Sewgobind at Eye for Games, Ramona Picenoni, Raphael Andres, Raúl Pellicier Villafaña, Red Ochsenbein, Reto Senn, Reto Silvano Eigenmann, Rick Adams, Robbert van Rooden, Roman Willi, Ron Müller, Sanae Hiraya, Sean Turner, Shruti Verma, Simon Legrand, Sophie Lamparter, Stéphane Siviero, Stéphanie Mader, Stefano Mersi, Supriya Suri and Nitesh Rohit and the lovely team at TokioGa, Sylvain Gardel, Tanima Maniktala Sachdev, Thomas Crausaz, Thomas Frei, Thomas Ott, Tobias Kopka, Tomi Prezigalo, Toshifumi Nakabayashi, Toshio Ishibashi, Tracey McCulloch, Tristan Donovan, Victor Manrique, Victoria Craven, Vijay Sinha, Zofia Glazer and, not least, my loving and supportive family.

Thank you!

Author

Chris Solarski is an artist game designer and author of the seminal book, *Drawing Basics and Video Game Art: Classic to Cutting-Edge Art Techniques for Winning Video Game Design.* He has lectured on emotions and storytelling in video games at international events including the Smithsonian Museum's landmark *The Art of Video Games* exhibition, SXSW, Game Developers Conference, and FMX. His projects at Solarski Studio continue to explore the intersections between video games, classical art, and film to develop new forms of player interaction and emotionally rich experiences in games.

Permissions

The author acknowledges the copyright owners of the games, motion pictures, and artwork that have been used in this book for purposes of commentary, criticism, and scholarship under the Fair Use Doctrine. Video game stills have been captured from gameplay footage created by the following YouTube users: Bolloxed, Boss Fight Database, GAME MOVE, GameRiot, Gamer's Little Playground, HassanAlHajry, Maximus Decimus Meridius, Mike Bettencourt, NiZZULiVE, Sandmans Gaming, Sly Shooter, theRadBrad, ToloDK, VivixGames, and xKrayZee.

Introduction

Video games come in many forms. Some lean toward pure gameplay—inspired by traditional games like chess—while others use gameplay as a medium to tell stories. The latter, *narrative-driven* variety, are essentially an accumulation of traditional artistic disciplines (visual art, scriptwriting, cinematography, music, animation, and physical performance) orchestrated through game design. A game designer defines the rules that govern how a particular game should be played by setting *goals* and imposing interesting *obstacles* that prevent the player from immediately achieving those goals. These two mechanisms—goals and obstacles—create the conflict that is at the heart of every story irrespective of the medium, be it film, animation, theater, opera, novels, or video games. Only with video games it is the player—and not the protagonist of the story—who must succeed through a mix of creative strategy, luck, and endurance.

Big budget franchises such as *The Last of Us* and *Grand Theft Auto* define our aesthetic expectations of what constitutes good video game storytelling. The enormous amount of work that goes into crafting such games—matched by the computational power of today's gaming consoles—has led to the creation of interactive stories and virtual worlds that we would have not thought possible when the medium was born in 1958 with the creation of *Tennis for Two* (Figure I.1). Despite these skyrocketing technical and artistic advances, we should nonetheless pause to reflect on whether games could deliver even more emotionally rich story experiences.

One cue for self-reflection comes in the form of the animation industry's parody of game characters in Walt Disney Pictures *Wreck-It Ralph* (2012), directed by Rich Moore (Figure I.2). In a world where good is always good and evil is always evil, Wreck-It Ralph rebels against established video game conventions by daring to reject his role as a video game villain and become a "good guy"—thus developing into a character with emotional *depth*. Although the film is clearly a comedy, it nonetheless presents us with a truth: video games are epitomized by

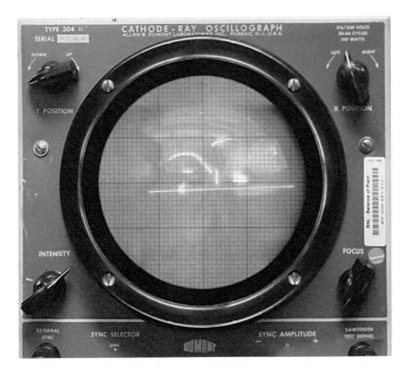

Figure I.1 *Tennis for Two* (1958), by American physicist, William Higinbotham, is considered to be the world's first video game that displayed visuals and game elements on-screen without the use of overlays.

Figure I.2 *Wreck-It Ralph* (2012), Walt Disney Animation Studios, directed by Rich Moore. Wreck-It Ralph's wish to become a good guy sends him on a spiritual journey that sees him develop into a more lifelike character with emotional depth.

simplistic characters that in other mediums would be described as emotionally *flat*. The prevalent level of character development in games can be summarized with the following quote on traditional fairy tales by Doug Lipman from his book, *Improving Your Storytelling: Beyond the Basics for All Who Tell Stories in Work or Play* (August House 1999):

> Traditional fairy tales … emphasize *actions* between flat characters with almost no depiction of internal states. They prefer the vast scope that includes beggars and queens, the completely good and utterly evil. … A central character may be transformed socially or physically but never internally.

Lipman could just as easily be writing about the majority of video game characters, who likewise fail to express a sense of complex inner feelings. *Cutscenes* (noninteractive animations often used to bookend segments of gameplay) certainly help to add a sense of emotional depth to video game characters but we have plenty of room for improvement when it comes to expression of meaningful emotions *in-game*—when the player is in control of proceedings (Figure I.3). If we wish to move forward and elicit complex emotions in our players that are on a par with music, film, and animation, then game art and game design must likewise make the same transformative journey as Wreck-It Ralph.

The success of storytelling in games depends on the entire development team—directors, game designers, artists, writers, programmers, and musicians—working in concert toward a singular artistic vision that celebrates emotional complexity and depth. In fact, we can liken the ideal game development process to that of a classical music orchestra consisting of many diverse musicians playing in harmony to a single music manuscript. However, the medium of video games is so young that we've yet to realize a common language that is equivalent to that of music and music notation.

Fortunately, the task is not as difficult as it may seem since we can inherit the rich history of craftsmanship from the artistic disciplines that games encapsulate—techniques that have been refined over thousands of years. Building from a foundation of art forms as varied as ancient Greek sculpture, classical

(a)   (b)

Figure I.3 (a) A noninteractive cutscene from *Uncharted 4: A Thief's End* (2016), by Naughty Dog, and (b) an in-game action moment where players are in control of the main protagonist, Nathan Drake.

painting and film, this book will define a framework that is mindful of gaming's principal relationship between player action, game design, game art, and audio. The roots of this framework are grounded in *primary shapes* and *dynamic composition*.

We will begin by exploring the aesthetic value of primary shapes: the circle, square, and triangle. Primary shapes are equivalent to musical notes—enabling us to modulate the emotional value of game art and interaction along an aesthetic scale. The second component, dynamic composition, will help us organize the complex visual and interactive systems of video games into eight simple elements: character shapes and poses, lines of movement, environment shapes, pathways, dialogue, framing, audio, and player gestures. We will use dynamic composition to analyze the ingredients that make award-winning games like *Journey, The Last of Us*, and Nintendo's *Super Mario* franchise so engaging.

Functioning much like musical chords, the combination of primary shapes and dynamic composition will enable us to pause video games at key moments during gameplay and make cross-section studies to understand how individual elements collectively define the player's overall aesthetic experience. Such a simple process for understanding video games is vital to fluency in video game storytelling and will set us in good stead for later chapters when we will analyze complex arrangements of dynamic composition in the context of the *dramatic curve* and *transitions*.

Transitions are the structural pillars of storytelling, which we'll use to analyze techniques for transmitting powerful scripted and player-driven stories that advocate gameplay and player agency. These sections will not teach you how to write a compelling narrative. Nor will they cover the full breadth of narrative theory. Rather, we will focus on the most common techniques for conveying story—like those of the proverbial storyteller sitting around the (digital) campfire. Brief examples from films will set the context for examining the do's and don'ts of storytelling techniques for video games, including *Gone Home, Minecraft*, and the *Grand Theft Auto* series.

For the sake of simplicity, the term "video games" used throughout this book includes any medium that contains an element of interactivity. In fact, you'll find that the timeless principles featured in the following pages can be applied to all art forms irrespective of the medium—serving as a common reference point for readers to apply their unique skill set. This book is therefore for developers of video games and virtual reality, filmmakers, gamification and transmedia experts, and everyone else interested in experiencing resonant and meaningful interactive stories. Furthermore, it is also up to players and video game critics to become more literate in the language of interactive storytelling, and set higher expectations, if the medium is to evolve toward its full potential.

How to Use This Book

Specialized knowledge of this topic is not required despite the advanced techniques featured in later chapters. Concepts are gradually introduced so that non-gamers, beginners, and seasoned game developers can benefit. Along the way, you'll find suggested notation for each element of dynamic composition. Make a quick study of each notation in a sketchbook using a pencil or ballpoint pen to help build your storytelling vocabulary. The suggested notation is deliberately simple enough so that nonartists should be comfortable sketching.

The final chapters contain a selection of examples from films and video games presented as sequences of stills. Because these mediums are best understood while in motion, I highly recommend making the effort to watch video footage of the scenes in question for which you'll find prompts throughout the book in the form of a *Replay* boxed text. A growing selection of video clips relevant to each chapter can be found at www.solarskistudio.com/videos. Better still is to play the featured video game sequences as playtesting is a vital part of developing your fluency in game art and interaction.

I

Primary Shapes and Dynamic Composition

Principles for the development of a complete mind. Study the science of art. Study the art of science. Develop your senses—especially learn how to see. Realize that everything connects to everything else.

Leonardo da Vinci (1452–1519)

In the following chapters we'll explore what are arguably the most effective design tools we have for shaping the aesthetic experience of a video game: primary shapes and dynamic composition. Our goal is to find a universal design language that is understood by individuals from all corners of the industry—including developers, academics, and consumers—and one that encompasses gaming's unique element of interactivity.

Three Primary Shapes

At the core of this language are the three primary shapes—the circle, square, and triangle—which can also be represented as lines (curved, straight, and angular lines) and forms (the *Platonic solids*: spheres and cylinders, boxes, and pyramids). For simplicity, I will refer to them collectively as primary shapes unless a specific reference is necessary (Figure SI.1).

Figure SI.1 The three primary shapes: the circle, square, and triangle are the basic components of humankind's instinctual and universally understood visual language.

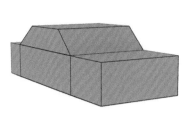  

Figure SI.2 The three primary forms are fundamental to sculpting and 3D modeling software where they are used as common starting points for both organic and designed objects: including trees, vehicles, and human figures.

The ancient Greek philosophers who invented the Platonic solids believed these forms constituted nature's building blocks and referred to them as *the roots of all things*. And rightly so! If you're a 3D artist you'll recognize these forms from modeling software applications like Blender, Maya, 3ds Max, and Cinema 4D, where they are generally referred to as *primitives*. Primitives are used as the basis for the development of an infinite variety of complex 3D objects. The process of modeling such objects always starts with the artist picking a primary shape that best approximates the final form before it's cut, stretched, extruded, and hewn into shape. For instance, a complex tree may start out as a combination of simple spheres and cylinders; box forms can be used to block-in a car; and the human head is often conceptualized as a combination of sphere and box forms (Figure SI.2).

Primary Shapes and Emotional Themes

What is especially interesting about primary shapes is that each corresponds to a particular set of high-level emotional themes that have remained constant throughout art history.

Associated Themes

Irrespective of an object's symbolic value, aligning its broader shape concept to the circle, square, or triangle will consequently align it to one of the following themes:

Circle: innocence, youth, energy, movement, positivity, freedom, relaxation

Square: maturity, balance, stubbornness, strength, rest, restraint, rational, conservative, calm

Triangle: aggression, force, instability, pain, sorrow, tension

Picture the three primary forms—the sphere, box form, and pyramid—placed on a table. Now imagine shaking that table. The round sphere would roll around, thus demonstrating its dynamic properties. The balanced cube and pyramid would remain in place. Now imagine if somebody threw the sphere and pyramid toward you for you to catch. You'd instinctively hesitate to catch the pyramid, even if you knew it wouldn't harm you, based on your learned automatic response to sharp objects, in contrast to soft and round shapes. Each of these objects can be interchanged with something that resembles the basic form—such as oranges, ancient Greek columns (that remain standing to this day!), and a thorny plant (Figure SI.3).

Why we associate these shapes with their corresponding themes has to do with our real-life experiences and the sense of *touch*. Touch is the first sensory system that fetuses develop in the womb over a year before the sense of sight becomes active and fully mature. Much of what we interpret about the world around us during childhood is learned through our touch senses. By feeling objects and comparing textures we quickly develop a mental shorthand for assessing the general characteristics of objects based on our tactile experiences. These learned instincts to primary shapes are part of humankind's survival mechanism. Paul Eckman, the renowned psychologist and expert on nonverbal communication, calls such phenomena *species-constant learning* because these are experiences that are consistent across all cultures. Sharp, triangular shapes are the most eye-catching because our survival instincts evolved to keep a wary lookout for anything that is potentially harmful to our well-being.

Although the number of themes may appear fairly limited, they are sufficiently broad to fit most aesthetic concepts that you'll encounter in life and art. This flexibility also ensures that each member of the development team—programmers, writers, artists, musicians, and game designers—can interpret them using their

Figure SI.3 From left to right: oranges (circle), ancient Greek columns (square), thorny plant (triangle).

Figure SI.4 Artists and designers exploit our universal experiences with touch in order to communicate with audiences through the three primary shape concepts in subjects as diverse as logos, architecture, pathways, and vehicles.

particular area of expertise. This versatility will become fundamental to the storytelling techniques we'll explore in subsequent chapters.

Irrespective of the design discipline, circle, square, and triangle shape concepts can be found embedded in every design discipline, although it's worth noting that their presence is often a subconscious solution to an artist's or designer's idea. Study the images in Figure SI.4 and imagine switching the shape concepts for each object. You'll find that the aesthetic impression for each object becomes completely at odds with what the designers likely intended. For example, would the circular Disney logo look as family-friendly if it featured the triangular font of thrash metal band, Anthrax? Would London's National Gallery or the Range Rover still project stability, safety, and sophistication if their balanced vertical and horizontal lines were replaced with circles? Would the Lamborghini lose its aggressive edge if it were designed with the rounded forms of the Volkswagen Beetle? While pathways create visual impressions as well as inspire us to walk, and thus feel, a particular way: from winding pathways in parks and places of relaxation, straight pathways for utilitarian journeys, and zigzagging pathways that we might associate with a treacherous trail on a steep mountain pass. It is no wonder that the philosopher, Plato (ca. 427–347 BC) stated, "Geometry is knowledge of the eternally existent."

The Shape Spectrum and Dynamic Composition

The emotional value of video game elements—including visual and nonvisual elements—are likewise influenced by the shape concept to which they are aligned. The consistency with which the circle, square, and triangle can be used to express certain themes allows us to orientate the primary shapes along a *shape*

Figure SI.5 The shape spectrum transitioning from a circle to a square and triangle, and accompanied iconic video game characters that embody the respective themes. From left to right: Kirby created by Masahiro Sakurai, Steve created by Markus "Notch" Persson, and Bowser created by Shigeru Miyamoto.

spectrum (Figure SI.5). Functioning much like a musical scale, the shape spectrum is a *comparative analysis* tool for assessing and manipulating the aesthetic alignment of individual design elements. Each shape can be used to amplify or subvert the emotional themes of a narrative.

Our shape spectrum works hand-in-hand with dynamic composition. "Composition" refers to the act of combining parts or elements to form a whole. In video game terms this refers to the component parts of a video game that occur at any one moment in an interactive experience. "Dynamic composition" implies that these gameplay *snapshots* can be varied from moment to moment to serve the aesthetic requirements of the story.

Unlike with traditional art forms, interactivity means that player actions are closely bound to the visual and artistic experience and must also be considered in the context of composition even though they occur outside the frame. The eight elements of dynamic composition include character shapes and poses, lines of movement, environment shapes, pathways, dialogue, framing, audio,

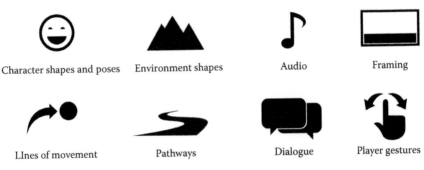

Character shapes and poses   Environment shapes   Audio   Framing

LInes of movement   Pathways   Dialogue   Player gestures

Figure SI.6 The eight elements of dynamic composition for organizing the complex arrangement of visual and nonvisual game elements.

The Eight Elements of Dynamic Composition

Character Shapes and Poses
Lines of Movement
Environment Shapes
Pathways
Dialogue
Framing
Audio
Player Gestures

You can think of dynamic composition as the fundamental elements needed for the *whiteboxing* stage of development—the preliminary prototype stage where key game elements are blocked-in with simple shapes and placeholders to test if the basic design supports the desired gameplay experience before final art assets are created. It's upon this foundation of dynamic composition that layers of detail will be added (light, color, voice acting, animation, etc.) by the various disciplines.

and player gestures (Figure SI.6). An important consideration for video game design is that each element of dynamic composition is pervasive—meaning that it is consistently present during gameplay—to ensure that players are always aware of it despite a constantly changing viewpoint within the game world.

Summary

The real world tactile-basis of primary shapes means that they are a timeless feature of art, allowing us to find relationships between seemingly disparate artistic disciplines that even include sound and nonvisual communication. Over the course of the next eight chapters we will sequentially examine each element of dynamic composition through the lens of our primary shape concepts and their respective themes, which are summarized as positive (circle), neutral (square), and negative (triangle). Dynamic composition will give us the necessary framework to orchestrate complex interactive stories and aesthetic experiences explored in later chapters with the dramatic curve and transition techniques.

⬤ Character Shapes and Poses

This chapter will explore how primary shapes and the shape spectrum featured in Section I can help us make sense of the first element of dynamic composition: character shapes and poses. We will investigate the increased narrative possibilities of dynamic character shapes and poses, which must adapt to the aesthetic needs of the story.

Iconic Character Design

A person's gestures—the positions their body assumes when they sit, stand, or walk—are an immense clue to their personality or current emotional state. You can witness these clues from the way people hunch their shoulders and tense their muscles when stressed versus the visibly languid state of someone in relaxation. Or, consider a ballerina striking a delicate pose mid-performance alongside a boxer before a bout. Although video game characters exist within a virtual, make-believe world, designing them requires the same sensitivity to gestures as if they were real people. The characters in Nintendo's *Super Mario* series are a prime case study for the role of primary shapes in character design because they are designed with a Japanese minimalist sensibility.

How would you describe Mario's personality? Dynamic, youthful, and positive come to mind—words that align with the emotional themes of the circle. It is therefore no surprise to find that everything about Mario's design is based on the circle shape concept (Figure 1.1), from his rounded shoes up to his spherical ears. Even his pose is arced like a ballerina to suggest a larger circle to convey his buoyant personality. The design of Mario's exterior shape concept gives us a strong sense of who he is on the inside.

Figure 1.1 Nintendo's Mario aligns to the circle shape concept, which is visible in the character's spherical body and curved gesture.

How about Mario's brother, Luigi? Rather than design Luigi from scratch, the artists at Nintendo took Mario's iconic design as a template and stretched it vertically—giving Luigi a decidedly taller overall shape that reflects his pillar-like supporting role as Mario's sidekick (Figure 1.2). These references to a rectangle externalize Luigi's personality through the emotional themes associated with the square shape concept.

At the other end of the shape spectrum we find Mario's antagonist, Wario, who is aligned to the aggressive triangle shape concept (Figure 1.3). Mario's timeless design has again been used as a starting template for Wario. Ignoring the obvious difference in Wario's waistline, the artists at Nintendo have adroitly done little more than dial his shoes, eyes, moustache, nose, and ears toward the triangle end of the shape spectrum in visual contrast to Mario's circular motif. Wario's

Figure 1.2 Luigi from Nintendo is a taller version of Mario's character design—depicted here in an upright pose that references the balanced square shape concept.

Figure 1.3 Nintendo's design for Wario demonstrates what happens when Mario's spherical shapes are dialed to an aggressive, triangle shape concept.

arms—posed and tensed like a boxer's—also reference the edgy lines of a lightning bolt. In fact, you'll find that almost every enemy within the Mario universe aligns to the triangle shape concept.

Psychological Gestures

Mario, Luigi, and Wario's designs demonstrate how the shape spectrum of emotions can help designers to tune their characters to communicate positive, neutral, and negative personalities, respectively. Because all three characters derive from Mario's character template, they could essentially represent the same character in different emotional states! Their respective poses likewise reference a concept known as *psychological gestures*—termed by the great Russian playwright, actor, and teacher, Anton Chekhov (1860–1904)—to describe the physical expression of a character's thoughts, feelings, and desires encapsulated in one movement or pose. A psychological gesture or pose, once defined, should inform every animation of the character. The design process of dialing an object's visual concept along the shape spectrum can be applied to every element of a video game (or the real world). Whether it's a tree, vehicle, building, or pathway—an object's silhouette can be rounded, straightened, or sharpened to create the same aesthetic effects.

Group Shapes

Large groups can also be designed in a similar fashion to individual characters, as in the *Total War: Rome* series by Creative Assembly (Figure 1.4). The series' game mechanics allow players to adjust army unit formations into various shapes including: the Cantabrian formation that has cavalry galloping around in a dynamic circle while firing arrows; square formations that balance unit defenses from all sides and; triangular wedge formations, which are effective at piercing enemy frontlines.

Simple Silhouette Concepts for Intricate Characters

Shape concepts are a fundamental consideration of character design even when dealing with more intricate and "realistic" characters. This is because a person or

Figure 1.4 The circle, square, and triangle are put to military use in *Total War: Rome II* (2013), by Creative Assembly—demonstrating that the shapes of large groups share aesthetic qualities with individual characters.

well-designed character can be distinguished by their silhouette alone, without the need for supporting details. As you can see from the *Final Fantasy XIV* (2010) character silhouettes (Figure 1.5), shape concepts combined with variations on size, proportions, body shapes and costumes aptly communicate the essence of each

Figure 1.5 Characters from *Final Fantasy XIV* (2010), by Square Enix, annotated with simplified silhouettes that illustrate how the essence of each character is transmitted through their shape concept.

character—ranging from a playful spherical concept to a pillar-like powerhouse and triangular antagonist.

Dynamic Character Poses

Disney animators from animation's Golden Age made a point of expressing the changing emotions and motivations of characters to make them appear more life-like. The animated sequence from *Snow White and the Seven Dwarfs* (1937), by Walt Disney, captures Grumpy's reaction to an affectionate kiss from Snow White (Figure 1.6). Notice how, from right to left, the aggressive angularity of his pose, erect hat, and facial expression (triangle shape concept) gradually transform into softer, curved forms as his temper dissipates (circle), before coming to a defiant, upright stop once he regains his self-control (square). More importantly, the sequence of poses creates a powerful illusion that the character is thinking because of the transition between two aesthetically different emotions. Without the change of attitude, Grumpy would appear emotionally two-dimensional and flat. Influential artist and leader of the French Romantic School, Eugène Delacroix (1798–1863), made similar observations about people when he wrote: "There may be ten different people in one [person], and sometimes all ten appear within a single hour."

Video game characters should also adopt poses to communicate their changing emotional and physical state. However, dynamic character poses are extremely complex and time-consuming to implement in a gameplay context when dealing with a realistic aesthetic, which makes them very costly. At the big-budget end of game development we have games like *Rise of the Tomb Raider* (2015), by Crystal

Figure 1.6 Grumpy in *Snow White and the Seven Dwarfs* (1937), by Walt Disney. Sequence animated by Bill Tytla. From right to left, you can see how Grumpy's changing pose communicates what he is thinking—from an aggressive, triangular strut to a bashful arc before coming to a defiant, pillar-like stop.

Dynamics. Figure 1.7 illustrates some of the varied gestures we see Lara Croft perform within the first hour of gameplay, including a delirious and languid walk (circle concept), an upright and purposeful pose as she explores an ancient cave (square concept), and a rigid, icy huddle in the midst of a snow blizzard (triangle concept).

Expensive motion-captured performances are not necessary for character expression. Rae—the playable character in *Beyond Eyes* (2015) by Dutch developer Tiger & Squid—has only two principle poses to communicate when she's confident and happy (circle shape concept) versus when she's feeling anxious (triangle shape concept) (Figure 1.8). Players of *Beyond Eyes* nonetheless experience a strong sense of empathy for Rae despite her limited set of animation.

Figure 1.7 Lara Croft in *Rise of the Tomb Raider* (2015), by Crystal Dynamics, conveys her emotional and physical state through animations that help heighten player empathy.

Figure 1.8 In *Beyond Eyes* (2015), by Tiger & Squid, the protagonist's pose is upright and open when she's happy, and tight and closed when she's sad or apprehensive, as she embraces herself for comfort and walks timidly.

Equally, in the opening sections of *Journey* the playable character has a relatively upright posture and can jump freely and gracefully. But we witness a shift in the character's physical state as it's guided toward the final portion of the game atop the storm-shrouded mountain where it staggers forward, bent-over-double, against the pounding winds (Figure 1.9). *Thomas Was Alone* (2012)—featured in

Figure 1.9 The playable character in *Journey* (2012), by thatgamecompany, convincingly responds to changing narrative conditions—demonstrating a lifelike sense of struggle, while remaining a mysterious personality throughout the game.

Character Shapes and Poses Notation

If you're a video game developer you may wish to use the notation above to aid your team in discussing dynamic character shapes and poses. The icons are variations on the familiar smiley emoticon.

Chapter 2, Player-Character Empathy section—additionally demonstrates how even a minimalist aesthetic can convey a wide range of character emotions.

Summary

Primary shapes enable us to evaluate character designs objectively, while the details—the choice of clothing and props, for instance—tend to be culture-specific and therefore subjective. From self-funded indie to big budget games, imbuing characters with depth and complexity is vital to raising the level of story-telling in video games. We've learned how our primary shape concepts can influence the development of characters with emotional depth that go beyond video game conventions (e.g., circles are good and triangles are evil). However, considering the fast pace of many video games, it's often beneficial to be explicit and avoid confusing players with ambiguous characters. Shape concepts can also be combined for further variety. For example, an aggressive triangular theme can be tempered with rounded corners to better fit the softer aesthetics of a children's game.

Because playable characters are always visible on-screen, such design considerations have a powerful and continued emotional effect on the player-audience throughout gameplay. Artists on the development team can complement each shape concept with considerations for textures (soft, straight, and rough textures) and color (analogous, monochromatic, and complementary color schemes). Closely bound to how we perceive a character and its shape and pose is the character's animation in terms of jump arcs and lines of movement, which we'll explore in the next chapter.

2 Lines of Movement

A video game character's lines of movement are the player's primary means of expression because they determine the mode of movement within the game's virtual space. For the purpose of storytelling in games we are less concerned with movements of a character's hand or facial expressions, for instance, because such animations are often too subtle to be noticed in the midst of action, on a character that takes up a small percentage of total screen space. Our primary concern is for broader animations that remain readable at every resolution, which includes character jump arcs and lines of movement. Before we explore the aesthetic effects of movement, we must make an important distinction between the two principle forms of character interaction: *guided* and *synchronized* characters.

Guided versus Synchronized Characters

Character controls for games like Ustwo's *Monument Valley* (2014) fall into the category of *guided* characters (Figure 2.1). What this means is that players' actions are not synchronized with the character. Rather, the player must first tap on the screen to specify a target destination toward which the playable character automatically walks along a predefined path. The player must wait passively until the character reaches its destination, which gives them time to contemplate solutions to the beautifully realized environment puzzles.

Synchronized characters are controlled by having players use gestures that imitate the character's movements, as in Figure 2.2 from *Lara Croft GO* (2016), by Square Enix Montreal. The game's design—led by Swiss game director Daniel Lutz—is more action-orientated than ustwo's, *Monument Valley*. As a result, players of *Lara Croft GO* must swipe left to have Lara Croft move left and swipe right if they wish for her to

Figure 2.1 *Monument Valley* (2014), by ustwo, is an example of interaction using guided characters, where character movement is largely automated after an action has been triggered by the player.

move right. Of the two interaction types—guided and synchronized—synchronized characters have the greater scope to generate player-character empathy because they allow players to physically embody the character's movements, even if the action is abstracted to swipes of the finger on a smartphone or controller. This ability for players to physically mimic actions that are presented in the artwork is what makes video games such an exhilarating storytelling medium. We will therefore focus on examining synchronized characters and how our shape spectrum of emotions can be applied to their animations to alter the aesthetic experience of interaction.

The Shape of Movement

When a player presses the jump button in the opening and closing levels of *Journey*, the playable character jumps gracefully across the screen. The implied line that this jump arc creates—emphasized by the character's trailing scarf—is aesthetically aligned to a sine wave and the circle shape concept. *Journey*'s development team took inspiration from the movements of sea creatures to imbue the game's playable character with an equally delicate grace (Figure 2.3).

Figure 2.2 *Lara Croft GO* (2016), by Square Enix Montréal, features a synchro-nized character that is controlled by having players mirror its movements using approximate gestures.

Figure 2.3 Lines of movement of the playable character in *Journey*, by that-gamecompany, suggest curved lines that are implicitly drawn across the screen in response to the player's input.

Speed, Line Tension, and Continuity of Movement

Mario's jump arcs in games like *New Super Mario Bros. U* (2012), by Nintendo, are also aligned to the circle shape concept. This puts Mario in the same aesthetic category as *Journey*'s character. However, a significant contributing factor to the look and feel of movement is *speed*, *line tension*, and *continuity of movement*. We can see from Figure 2.4 that the line tension of Mario's curved jump arc is much tighter and his movements faster than *Journey*'s character. Staggered or intermit-tent motions add further aesthetic modulation, in contrast to continuous movement.

Lines of movement that reference the square shape concept tend to be found in side-scrolling platform games. A progressive example of this genre is *INSIDE*, by Danish developer Playdead. *INSIDE* (2016) takes place in a dystopian world pre-sented through gameplay sections requiring conformist, linear movements along horizontal or vertical pathways (Figure 2.5).

Figure 2.4 Although Mario's jump arcs in *New Super Mario Bros. U* (2012), by Nintendo, are in the same aesthetic category as *Journey*, they have a slightly different look and feel due to variations in character speed, line tension, and continuity of movement.

Figure 2.5 The protagonist of *INSIDE* (2016), by Playdead, often moves in straight lines along horizontal pathways and vertical ladders, which underscore the regimented dystopia of the game's setting.

Figure 2.6 The zigzagging, triangular lines of movement of Sam Gideon in *Vanquish* (2010), by PlatinumGames, allow players to physically empathize with the aggressive actions of the playable character.

The animations of Sam Gideon—the playable character from *Vanquish* (2010), by PlatinumGames—sit at the triangular end of the shape spectrum (Figure 2.6). In contrast to *Journey*'s traveler, Sam Gideon jolts around the environment like a pinball when players activate his boost function. The increase in speed demands that players make more frequent and abrupt adjustments to the character's trajectory as he zigzags around the environment. Imagine how *Journey*, *INSIDE*, and *Vanquish* would look and feel if the lines of movement for each game were interchanged. Make a mental note of these lines of movement, as they are central to the concept of melody and pitch contours, which we will explore in Chapter 7, Melody and Lines of Movement section.

Communicating Personality with the In-Game Camera

In the absence of an on-screen character, we must imagine that the camera represents the perspective of a living-breathing person capable of expressing a whole range of emotions that can be aligned to one of our primary shapes. Consider the run speed, turn speed, camera height, and control responsiveness in the opening section of *Killzone Shadow Fall* (2013), by Guerrilla Games, where the first-person playable character is a child called Lucas Kellan. In later levels, players take control of an older Lucas, whose general movements feel more aggressive and supercharged by comparison (Figure 2.7). The resulting impression is that of piloting two emotionally differing characters whose presence can occasionally be implied by a shadow cast onto the environment.

An additional element to consider is how the in-game camera behaves in relation to the character's lines of movement. Most games feature a camera that has been stabilized to remove distracting camera shake. Not so for the *Gears of War* franchise by Epic Games, which features a camera that bounces according to the player's footsteps when sprinting (Figure 2.8). The combined effect of the character's animation and camera shake creates a sense of realism and aggression that is perfectly suited to the brutal theme of the franchise. The same camera effect can be used to emphasize impacts—such as the action of firing a weapon or being hit—although these should be used in moderation since they can lead to nausea in some players.

Figure 2.7 *Killzone Shadow Fall* (2013), by Guerrilla Games, starts with the player embodying the young Lucas Kellan before taking control of his adult form—a switch that is reflected in the relative height of the first-person camera and walk animation speed.

Figure 2.8 *Gears of War* (2006), by Epic Games, features a camera that bounces in time with the playable character's footsteps when sprinting, which creates a realistic sense of presence.

Player-Character Empathy

In contrast, the visually enchanting *Beyond Eyes* (2015) restricts movement to a ponderous walk that reflects the predicament of the blind protagonist, Rae, as she searches for her cat. Without this imposed slow pace, players would never achieve empathy for the character (Figure 2.9).

Figure 2.9 *Beyond Eyes* (2015), by Tiger & Squid, features a character with a leisurely pace, which deliberately slows progression through the game to heighten player-character empathy.

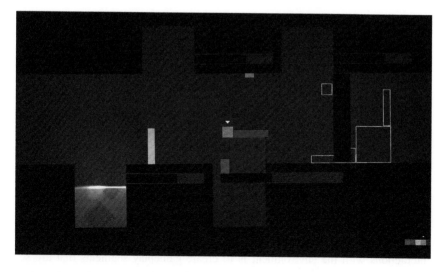

Figure 2.10 *Thomas Was Alone* (2012), by Mike Bithell, features five characters that include the main protagonist, Thomas (short red rectangle), who can only jump to a medium height; John (thin yellow rectangle) bounces like a spring and can jump very high; while Claire (large blue rectangle) can barely lift herself off the ground but has the ability to float.

Animations need not be elaborate to communicate a convincing sense of personality, as illustrated in the award-winning platform puzzle game, *Thomas Was Alone* (2012), by Mike Bithell. The game features five playable characters that are presented as simple colored rectangles (Figure 2.10). The personality of each character is primarily transported through varied shape proportions and animations. Switching between characters results in players having to adjust their physical gestures to match the changing animations and character abilities. We could conceivably take the cast of five characters from *Thomas Was*

Replay

Thomas Was Alone (2012), by Mike Bithell
Publisher: Mike Bithell, Curve Studios, and Bossa Studios
   Play through *Thomas Was Alone* until you've unlocked all five characters. Take turns with each character to navigate around the environment and get a feeling for how the respective animations influence your physical movements and sensations. Alternatively, use the search term "Thomas Was Alone Walkthrough" on YouTube to review gameplay footage—imagining a light trail behind the characters as each jumps, slides, or floats around the screen under the player's control.

Alone and combine them into an individual personality that changes its mood over the course of a narrative.

Dynamic Character Animations and Level Design

Dynamically changing a character's animations over the course of a game comes with consequences that can be very costly to address (Figure 2.11). A character's personality—as expressed through its set of abilities and lines of movement—is typically the domain of the game designers. If a game's story demanded that, say, Mario switches from his usual upbeat and bouncy self to an aggressive and vengeful character akin to *Ninja Gaiden*'s, Ryu Hayabusa, the emotional change would have to be reflected in his broader movements. The angular, slashing jumps that he would consequently perform would affect gameplay, determining whether he can successfully reach certain platforms and avoid pitfalls.

One solution to ensure that changing a character's animations doesn't break interactions with the environment is to create gameplay segments that are set apart from the normal action—much like a musical interlude in music. Lead designer, Richard Lemarchand, did just that for Chapter 18 of *Uncharted 3: Drake's Deception* (2011), by Naughty Dog, where the player controls an increasingly weakened and staggering Nathan Drake (Figure 2.12). All the usual parkour-style obstacles associated with *Uncharted* games have been left out, thus removing the player's impulse to jump and climb. The change in pace of the character's animations for this scene creates a powerful emotional contrast to an otherwise action-packed game.

A more costly but effective solution for implementing dynamic animations is to adapt the environment to the playable character's changing abilities, as in games like *Journey*. The presence of platforms in *Journey*'s environments always coincides with segments of the game where the traveler can jump and glide (Figure 2.13). The platforms are absent whenever the character's movements

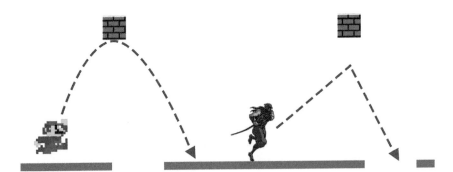

Figure 2.11 Changing a character's animations can have drastic consequences for gameplay—affecting whether characters can successfully navigate an environment that must strictly adhere to a consistent unit system that defines the size and placement of props.

Figure 2.12 Chapter 18: The Rub' al Khali in *Uncharted 3: Drake's Deception* (2011), by Naughty Dog, takes place in a desert environment that is void of obstacles, which allowed designers to insert special animations for the physically exhausted Nathan Drake without disturbing the delicate gameplay system experienced in the bulk of the game.

Figure 2.13 Platforms in *Journey* (2012), by thatgamecompany, are present when the playable character has the ability to jump and glide (left) and are absent when the character becomes grounded (right).

become grounded—such as when it begins its ascent of the windy mountaintop. The obvious danger with such a design approach is that certain areas of the environment may become inaccessible to the player depending on the character's abilities at any one time. Which is why this approach often requires that customized environment props are used in place of modular elements that could otherwise be reused in different parts of the game.

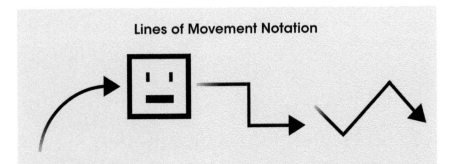

Lines of Movement Notation

The suggested notation for discussing character movement, features lines that reference circle, square, or triangle shape concepts. The lines of movement can be dynamically modulated to elicit varied aesthetic sensations from players.

Summary

The delivery of an interactive story can only ever be as fluid as the character's animations—hence the reason why a large percentage of development work for narrative-driven games goes into creating polished and fluid animations. The notation in "Lines of Movement Notation" will enable every person—irrespective of their specialization (and artistic talent!)—to sketch movement concepts. It's vital that a character's animations align to the shape concept that best conveys their emotional state at any one time. Character movements are so pivotal to a game's story that you could conceivably remove everything else from a game and a narrative would still exist based on the changing lines of movement.

On a subtler level, *frame rate*—the frequency at which images of a video game are refreshed—can also be used to aesthetically modulate lines of movement. For instance, a frame rate of 30 frames-per-second (fps) is perfectly acceptable for gameplay. However, when compared alongside a frame rate of 60 fps, the slower 30 frames per second gives animations a more rugged, rougher sensation. While a frame rate of 60 fps appears more fluid and smoother.

The elements of dynamic composition that we've explored thus far—character shapes and poses, and lines of movement—are character-centric and therefore represent an extension of the player inside the virtual space. The following two elements of dynamic composition—environment shapes and pathways—define the dramatic stage for playable character's movements by setting obstacles and defining the flow of gameplay. We will first examine environment shapes, which concern the playable character's immediate surroundings and the aesthetic effects of character-environment relationships.

3 Environment Shapes

A character's surroundings are an important consideration for a game's visual composition because the environment takes up much of the image within the picture frame. For our purposes, the environment also includes secondary characters (both friendly and hostile nonplayable characters) and props. Environment objects collectively serve as narrative obstacles and constraints that act in harmony or in opposition to the playable character. Because of this close relationship between characters and the environment, it is beneficial to study the two elements side-by-side to determine character-environment relationships.

Harmony and Dissonance

The illustrations in Figure 3.1 represent characters placed in various environments. A circular character in a circular environment (Figure 3.1a) creates a sense of *harmony* because the character's shape concept is echoed in its surroundings. We also get a sense of harmony if both the character and environment are square, or triangular (Figure 3.1b). A character appears to be at home whenever its shape concept is echoed in the surrounding environment because the two elements share the same visual DNA.

We get a sense of *dissonance* when character and environment shapes contrast each other. A circular character appears threatened when placed in an edgy, triangular environment (Figure 3.1c), while a triangular character appears to be the threatening element in a soft and circular environment (Figure 3.1d).

The *Super Mario Galaxy* series of games by Nintendo is a great example of how this character-environment relationship works in practice. In Chapter 1, we studied Mario's circular character design concept. In *Super Mario Galaxy*, his

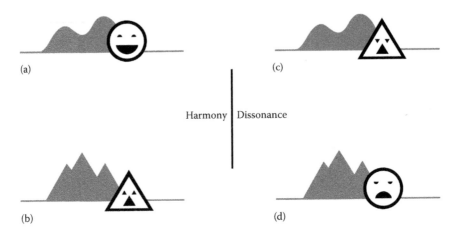

(a)

(c)

Harmony | Dissonance

(b)

(d)

Figure 3.1 A character appears to be at home when its visual DNA is echoed in its surroundings (a and b), and a sense of dissonance or threat is created when the surrounding environment has a different visual theme (c and d).

circular motif is echoed throughout his home world and his physical proportions also inform the design of buildings and props (Figure 3.2).

Mario appears out of place, in foreign territory, the instant he transitions to an environment that is not aligned to his circular theme (Figure 3.3). The shape contrast also applies to Mario's enemies that, like Wario, always feature elements that align with the triangle shape concept. *Super Mario Galaxy*'s character-environment shape design is so clear and distinct that we can reduce the games implied narrative

Figure 3.2 Mario's home planet in *Super Mario Galaxy* (2007), by Nintendo, echoes the circular shapes of his character design—creating character-environment harmony and a distinct sense of home and belonging.

Figure 3.3 The Bonefin Galaxy from *Super Mario Galaxy 2* (2010), by Nintendo, demonstrates the aesthetic dissonance created whenever the environment contains props and characters that contrast Mario's spherical shape concept.

to a dramatic clash of shapes in which a spherical Mario lives in a spherical universe overrun with triangular enemies that create a sense of dissonance. It's the player's role to clear the galaxy of triangles in order to restore harmony between circular Mario and his circular home environment.

Character-Centric Design

Blizzard Entertainment's design process also exemplifies the importance of strong character-environment shape concepts. With so many character races in the *World of Warcraft* (2004) universe, it is imperative that each new addition is visually distinct from others. For this reason, Blizzard uses a character-centric approach to developing each new race, which starts with the design of lead characters whose silhouettes must be easily distinguishable—even when viewed as black and white silhouettes, void of details. Work on the environment commences only once the race's character designs are finalized. Rather than start the design process anew, artists copy elements from characters and paste them into the environment—such as the triangular motifs seen in the environments belonging to the Warlords of Draenor (Figure 3.4). The shared shape concept for the warlords and their environment ensures that players instantly recognize the race's respective territory. To create a sense of dissonance, a character from a rival race with a different shape concept need only enter the territory and it will instantly be recognized as an outsider.

A similar sense of harmony and dissonance can be elicited by varying the relationship between a character's design (see Chapter 1, Character Shapes and Poses) and its lines of movement (see Chapter 2). Characters with a circular appearance and flowing lines of movement will be perceived as harmonious, while a

Figure 3.4 Environments belonging to the Warlords of Draenor in *World of Warcraft* (2004), by Blizzard Entertainment, were created by echoing elements of the triangular aesthetic of character designs in associated buildings to clearly convey the race's territory.

Figure 3.5 The skull motif of the *Gears of War* logo, by Epic Games, is echoed throughout the game in the chest armor of Marcus Fenix and the COG troops; in the faces of enemies; and level designs (notice the abstract eye sockets, nose, and mouth of the Trenches multiplayer map).

character with the same friendly appearance but with edgy lines of movement will create an unsettling, dissonant feeling.

Image Systems

A highly sophisticated example of character-environment shape relationships is illustrated by the *image system* embedded in the design of the *Gears of War* series by Epic Games (Figure 3.5). Filmmaker Gustavo Mercado defines image systems as "the use of recurrent images and compositions [...] that add layers of meaning to a narrative." The image system used in *Gears of War* starts with the franchise's logo that—as every well-designed logo should—summarizes the essence and values of the experience in one poignant, visual statement that serves to subliminally reiterate the overarching theme of annihilation.

The Architectural Value of Secondary Characters

The reason that secondary characters are conceptually grouped together with environment shapes is illustrated in the screenshot from *Grand Theft Auto V*

Figure 3.6 The above car pileup in *Grand Theft Auto V* (2013), by Rockstar Games, illustrates the architectural value of secondary characters, and the reason why they are grouped together with environments in dynamic composition.

(2013) in Figure 3.6. Consider that the vehicles are driven by artificial intelligence (AI) characters and are usually on the move. When vehicles become stationary, as in the traffic pileup, it becomes easier to understand their architectural value as they define the boundaries of the player's environment like a wall or building. Increasing or decreasing the amount of secondary characters or vehicles can therefore serve to modulate the intensity of navigating an environment by creating free, open spaces contrasted by tight, angular corridors. Additionally, if secondary characters move with gentle, curving motions, then the player's interaction will consequently be gentler. Enemy characters will naturally elicit more aggressive movements from the player.

Character-Environment Scale

Another aesthetic effect derived from character-environment relationships is the manipulation of relative scale. This happens throughout *Alice: Madness Returns* (2011)—a game in which the player feels vulnerable when Alice shrinks to a small size and powerful when she towers above the environment (Figure 3.7). A similar concept can be found in Respawn Entertainment's, *Titanfall* (2014), in which gameplay constantly shifts between fighting as a foot soldier, and piloting giant mechs.

The amount of space between the playable character, and secondary characters and props can also be modulated to create feelings of closeness or loneliness. Small spaces will naturally feel more intimate, although they can also feel claustrophobic if they become too small in relation to the playable character. The technique of varying spatial scale is used to great effect in *The Beginner's Guide*

Figure 3.7 *Alice: Madness Returns* (2011), by Spicy Horse, features a game mechanic that allows Alice to change her size relative to the environment, which makes the player feel vulnerable when Alice is small, and empowered when she is big.

(2015), by Davey Wreden at Everything Unlimited Ltd. Smaller environments have a comforting human scale, which is juxtaposed by big open spaces that verge on the sublime—giving players a sense of tragic loneliness, isolation, or of being exposed (Figure 3.8). *Journey,* by thatgamecompany, also uses the sense of detachment in large open spaces to make encounters with secondary players feel more meaningful and welcome.

Figure 3.8 *The Beginner's Guide* (2015), by Davey Wreden at Everything Unlimited Ltd., contrasts environments that go from small and intimate to large and inhospitable.

Replay

The Beginner's Guide (2015), by Everything Unlimited Ltd.
Publisher: Everything Unlimited Ltd.

   The Beginner's Guide is a revolutionary game and a masterclass in interactive storytelling. It can be completed in around 90 minutes, so even the most time-strapped readers should find a moment to play through. While playing, note how small spaces make you feel compared to wide-open environments.

Deductive Reasoning through Changing Locations

In addition to varying the environment scale for aesthetic effect, *The Beginner's Guide* demonstrates the importance of varying aesthetics between locations (Figure 3.9). The game's narrator guides players through a sequence of short video game vignettes—offering his personal interpretation as to their meaning and inviting players to draw their own conclusions. A series of varied environments will automatically prompt players to construct their own story and search for meaning in the sequence even if no explicit narrative is communicated. If we were to take the same environments but order them in a different sequence, a different interpretation would be generated. In the words of film director Stanley Kubrick, "A film [or video game] is—or should be—more like music than like fiction. It should be a progression of moods and feelings. The theme, what's behind the emotion, the meaning, all that comes later."

Figure 3.9 Changing the setting of a narrative automatically leads the player-audience to extract a personal interpretation of the narrative—which is an engaging phenomenon central to *The Beginner's Guide*, by Everything Unlimited Ltd.

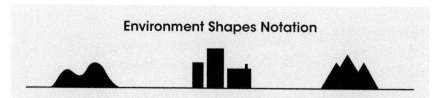

Environment Shapes Notation

A straightforward city silhouette or mountain range can be used for environment shape notation. Refer to the notation for character shapes and poses in Chapter 1 for indicating secondary characters.

Summary

The three elements of dynamic composition that we've explored thus far—character shapes and poses, lines of movement, and environment shapes—already demonstrate how a player's aesthetic experience can be altered using the shape spectrum. Our analysis uses the emotionally charged primary shapes—the circle, square, and triangle—as a comparative analysis tool to make sense of a wide variety of artistic styles and interactions. In practice, the simpler the shape concepts the easier it is for the player-audience to immerse themselves in a story.

We're about a third of the way to having a complete overview of dynamic composition, which will allow us to make snapshots of dynamic composition at any one moment of a game. In the next section, we will explore how pathways within a video game can shape the flow of player movement and influence the emotional experience of the player-audience in the context of a narrative.

4! Pathways

Pathways within an environment—just like the pathways in a park, or roads in a city—can readily be reduced to an abstract line concept. Whether a system of pathways is aligned to the circle, square, or triangle determines the visual pattern projected on-screen and the emotional effect on players. Where applicable, the following examples feature an aerial map alongside in-game screenshots to emphasize the relationship between 2D line concepts and 3D environments. The interactive aspect of video games also means that pathway shapes influence character movements and the player's gestures as they navigate the environment.

The Aesthetic Value of Pathway Lines

Take a moment to note the shape of pathways next time you visit a park or playground near your home. You'll likely find that the pathways are curved because the circle shape concept creates a gentle aesthetic quality appropriate for the activities intended for such areas. Rounded pathways also encourage pedestrians to walk in a leisurely manner even if they are only a visual suggestion and walking on the grass is permitted. The same is true for instances of curved pathways in video games illustrated by the environment from Liberty City in *Grand Theft Auto IV* (2008), whose gracefully curving pathways create a gentle driving experience (Figure 4.1).

The driving experience becomes edgier in *Grand Theft Auto IV* when the action shifts to a district with an angular system of roads. The acute angles of street junctions in Liberty City's Meat Quarter (Figure 4.2) mean that driving around corners requires sharper movements and sudden changes in direction. The amount of car traffic can be modulated to further increase angular behavior—as

Figure 4.1 A curving highway and the respective location on the Liberty City map from Rockstar North's, *Grand Theft Auto IV* (2008), illustrate the aesthetic relationship between pathways in 3D environments and their representation as 2D lines.

Figure 4.2 Road junctions with acute angles in Liberty City's Meat Quarter in *Grand Theft Auto IV* (2008), by Rockstar North, illustrate how pathways with a triangle shape concept generate a more aggressive driving experience.

Replay

Grand Theft Auto series, by Rockstar North
Publisher: Rockstar Games

Load-up your favorite *Grand Theft Auto* game and drive around the city paying close attention to how pathway lines presented in the user interface's mini map affect the handling of your vehicle. Alternatively, you're welcome to search for "GTA 5 City Tour" on YouTube to review gameplay footage, although you'll miss out on the physical feeling associated with pathway shape concepts.

Figure 4.3 Straight pathways in *Grand Theft Auto V* (2013), by Rockstar North, create a relatively dull driving experience compared to circular or angular pathways—assuming there are no other vehicles or obstacles on the road.

we explored in Chapter 3 (Figure 3.5)—because players must weave left and right to avoid oncoming vehicles.

When gameplay is set in an environment with long, straight pathways, the aesthetic experience becomes substantially calmer—assuming that there are no vehicles or obstacles to avoid along the way (Figure 4.3). The majority of pathways that we encounter in real life going to and from school or work are likewise straight and align with the square shape concept. Straight pathways are functional and direct—free of visual noise and extraneous movement—and can therefore be used to create moments of rest in-between pathways that align to circle and triangle shape concepts.

Complimentary and Contrasting Pathways

Pathways can be designed to complement or work in opposition to a character's movements—much like the concepts of harmony and dissonance discussed in Chapter 3. For example, the aggressive and angular character animations of *Gears of War 3* (2011) seem completely at odds with the circular pathways of the fictional sports arena in the game's Thrashball level (Figure 4.4). The accompanying map further highlights the arena's circle shape concept.

Figure 4.4 The round pathways of the Thrashball multiplayer arena in *Gears of War 3* (2011), by Epic Games, creates an amusing contrast to the game's aggressive characters and animations.

Figure 4.5 The opening environment of *Journey* (2012), by thatgamecompany, features no explicit pathways whatsoever—giving players free rein to set their own route.

Open Canvas

Journey's opening environment has no explicit pathways whatsoever (Figure 4.5). We can fittingly apply the concept of an *open canvas* in such cases, since players have complete freedom to track their own route through the landscape. Without pathways, the aesthetic experience falls solely on the character's lines of movement. When pathways become more defined in later levels of *Journey*, they bring with them a feeling of constriction, which implies a narrative theme of freedom versus restraint.

Blocked Pathways and Gating

The counter to an open canvas is a blocked pathway, which is the outcome of a locked door or an impassable obstacle. Blocked pathways bring the action to a stop and raise dramatic tension as players are forced to find a solution to proceed. Blocked pathways often coincide with a technique called *gating*, where game designers can prevent players from progressing through a narrative until they have completed a given objective, performed a specific action, developed new skills, or acquired a special item.

One of the most memorable moments in *The Last of Us* uses a blocked pathway to create powerful drama by subverting the players' expectations. High walls or fences are encountered on several occasions by the game's protagonists, Joel and Ellie. These obstacles are equivalent to a door that must be unlocked, which Joel overcomes by summoning Ellie and giving her a leg-up (Figure 4.6a). However, on one occasion Ellie does not appear (Figure 4.6b) because she is lost in thought contemplating the coming end of their journey. This unexpected event goes against

(a)   (b)

Figure 4.6 *The Last of Us* (2013), by Naughty Dog, features high walls and fences that players "unlock" with the assistance of Ellie (a), who—for dramatic effect—is not always cooperative (b).

Pathway Notation

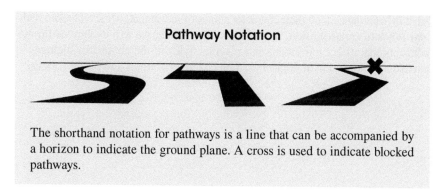

The shorthand notation for pathways is a line that can be accompanied by a horizon to indicate the ground plane. A cross is used to indicate blocked pathways.

previous instances of the same situation and therefore skillfully draws attention to the protagonists' close bond through gameplay—and not through a cutscene.

Summary

The video game examples in this chapter demonstrate principals to create aesthetic harmony or dissonance between character movement and environment pathways. Tension is modulated by varying the shape concepts of pathways, which, in turn, constrain players to certain lines of movement. Pathways need not align to the ground plane—such as the convoluted rollercoaster-like pathways of *Prince of Persia* (2008), by Ubisoft, which require spectacular gravity-defying

Figure 4.7 Pathways can be drawn across any part of the environment—not just the ground plane—as in the level design of *Prince of Persia* (2008) by Ubisoft.

wall runs, controlled slides, and carefully timed jumps to traverse paths that twist into all manner of shapes (Figure 4.7).

Removing pathways frees players to explore the environment any way they wish in accordance with their character's lines of movement, while a blocked pathway tends to create tension. In the following chapter, we will explore additional concepts that affect movement and playing styles in the context of dialogue—particularly nonverbal dialogue based on character abilities and player actions.

 Dialogue

The previous four elements of dynamic composition—character shapes and poses, lines of movements, environment shapes, and pathways—are easily discussed in the context of primary shapes because they concern visual art in the form of graphics and animation. The following three chapters feature elements of dynamic composition that concern less visual forms of communication: namely, dialogue, framing, and audio. The task of translating visual shape concepts to nonvisual elements becomes significantly easier if we permit ourselves, when necessary, to determine an emotional theme and then work backward to identify the primary shape concept associated with that particular emotion. The three primary shapes—the circle, square, and triangle—and their associated themes are reiterated here for convenience:

Circle: innocence, youth, energy, movement, positivity, freedom, relaxation

Square: maturity, balance, stubbornness, strength, rest, restraint, rational, conservative, calm

Triangle: aggression, force, instability, pain, sorrow, tension

Nonverbal Communication

Ever since the world's first video game, *Tennis for Two* (1958), games have espoused an unspoken dialogue based on actions over words. As the name suggests, *Tennis for Two* immersed two competitors in a virtual space in which they could serve and volley a sphere using controllers featuring buttons and rotating dials to adjust the angle of an invisible tennis racquet's swing. Words were abandoned within this virtual space in favor of an interactive dialogue made visible by the to-and-fro of the ball passing over the digital net. What made this dialogue possible was the result of the game's creator, William Higginbotham's, curated choice of physical inputs and virtual outputs. Little has changed in intervening years to alter this basic tenet of dialogue in games.

Playing a game for the first time is just like learning a new language. Through trial and error we test our expressive scope with a distilled set of tilt, tap, and swipe actions suited to the expressive needs of a particular interactive experience. Pressing a button in one game readies the playable character to aim and shoot, while the same button in another game prompts the character to grab the hand of a companion and guide her to safety. Through play we learn the specifics of nonverbal dialogue unique to each game—becoming fluent and more adept at expressing ourselves through practice. The following examples investigate this fundamental concept of dialogue in video games as well as more conventional notions of dialogue in the form of verbal and written communication. We will also explore how character abilities are defined through nonvisual customization settings and how they impact dialogue between players and secondary characters—starting with characters from the superstar indie title, *Minecraft* (2011).

Character Classes

To a video game programmer or game designer, the physical appearance of a character is of significantly less importance than the values that define the character's behavior. *Minecraft* is the perfect case study for character behavior because the game's uniform cube aesthetic allows us to focus on the nuances of behavior without becoming overly distracted by visual design. For instance, there is little to no difference in form and design between the *Minecraft* characters in Figure 5.1, beyond their surface textures, since they are all essentially

Figure 5.1 Behavior settings are the greatest differentiator between characters in the above lineup from *Minecraft* (2011), by Mojang—which consists of a default playable character (Alex), a Zombie, Zombie Pigman, and Skeleton.

composed of the same blocks. The most significant distinction is between the *class* to which each character belongs. The term class originates from role-playing games as a way to group characters with similar behavior, occupations, or by archetype. For example, Zombies belong to the hostile class of nonplayable characters that attack players on first sight while Zombie Pigmen belong to the neutral class that attacks only when provoked by the player. The following settings give us a glimpse of the finer level of attributes that drive each character's behavior:

The Player

Class: player

Objective: player-defined

Health points: 20

Armor points: vary

Attack strength: fist = 1, items = vary according to weapon

Zombie

Class: hostile

Objective: attack players and avoid hazards

Health points: 20

Armor points: 2

Attack strength (according to difficulty level): easy = 2, normal = 3, hard = 4

The full list of variables includes such options as speed, start location (*spawn point*), and items that are dropped when the character is killed. Although value differences between the playable character and Zombies may appear fairly subtle, complex and unexpected behaviors emerge once the characters are loaded into *Minecraft*'s open world and are free to roam and interact with their surroundings and each other. Secondary characters can have their settings modulated programmatically—such as objectives, strength, speed, and special abilities—if dramatic tension needs toning-down or ramping-up. These settings contribute to the personality of each character when coupled with concepts from Chapter 1, Character Shapes and Poses and Chapter 2, Lines of Movement that we explored previously. Whether the nonverbal dialogue that ensues between characters is friendly, neutral, aggressive, or a dynamic combination of all three aesthetics depends on what the game's designers choose to permit.

Skill Trees

Games with a role-playing component allow players to make their own choices about classes and special skills as they progress. To which class their character belongs is the top-level decision that players must make. *The Division* (2016), by Ubisoft, forgoes strict classification of character classes by giving players the option of three specializations that can be mixed and matched: medic, security, or tech abilities, which translate to healing (circle), supportive (square), and offensive (triangle) roles. The choice of abilities affects the character's style of play and role on the battlefield. Skills unique to each of these specializations allow players to customize their characters on a more granular level via a *skill tree* (Figure 5.2). As a result, a character that is strong in medic skills, for example, can be customized to have supplementary attributes from the security or tech classes. *The Division* allows players to manage their character's skills on the fly in response to changing gameplay situations. The more visual the effects of those choices, the more convincing the characters become. However, the subtle nature of character skills often makes them difficult to discern in the midst of combat, which is why skills are often enumerated or presented as icons via the user interface to visualize the nuanced inner workings of a character.

Character Customization

The ability to personalize and nurture a character means that players can become more emotionally invested in their digital avatars. Character customization allows players to modify the outward appearance of their playable character. The act of character customization can feel like a game in itself—as with the character

Figure 5.2 Skill trees in *The Division* (2016), by Ubisoft, allow players to fine-tune the attributes of their character, with new skill options becoming available as they progress through the game.

Figure 5.3 *Sunset Overdrive* (2014), by Insomniac Games, offers players a wide selection of clothing to adorn their characters with, so that everybody can personalize their flamboyant alter ego.

editor from *Sunset Overdrive* (2014), by Insomniac Games, which offers players a myriad of options to modify clothing and body features (Figure 5.3). Such cosmetic options are arguably less consequential than class and skill choices, but character customization is an important aspect of nonverbal dialogue because it offers players the possibility to express their alter ego and communicate through the concepts that we explored in Chapter 1.

Aesthetic Alignment of Dialogue

In the context of the shape spectrum, character classes can be organized according to their affinity to the playable character: positive and supportive characters align to the circle concept; neutral characters align to the square; and hostile characters to the triangle. The traits of Zombies in *Minecraft*, for instance, align exclusively with the triangle shape concept because they are designed to pursue players and inflict damage (although the *sandbox* nature of *Minecraft*'s gameplay means that enterprising players can always find a way to subvert established rules). Players and certain characters in the passive and neutral classes are more difficult to categorize because their aesthetic alignment can change dynamically from one moment to the next. For instance, pigs are predominantly passive (square)—wandering aimlessly while avoiding hazardous cliffs and water. However, pigs can also have assistive functions (circular)—such as being saddled and ridden by players carrying a carrot further down where indicated. Or they can turn into Zombie Pigmen if struck by lightning and become irrevocably hostile (triangular) if aggravated.

The greatest aesthetic modulation comes from players, who can direct *Minecraft*'s nonverbal dialogue at their will. Players can choose to play

Replay

Minecraft (2011), by Mojang
Publisher: Mojang
    Play a stint of *Minecraft* with a focus on nonverbal dialogue. In the context of the three primary shapes, try initiating a dialogue with fellow players or secondary characters based on different aesthetic themes. What can you communicate without resorting to the game's chat functionality?

harmoniously with nonthreatening classes and fellow gamers, by saddling a pig or assisting in mining and the building of structures with friends. Or they can be entirely neutral and nonengaging—avoiding character interactions to focus on their own, self-appointed errands. Players can also become disruptive by jeopardizing the efforts of others, slaughtering a pig for meat, or antagonizing an otherwise neutral spider, which triggers it to fight back.

Pictographic Communication of Mood and Intentions

In the absence of body language and nuanced facial expressions, a *Minecraft* player's mood and intentions can be discerned pictographically based on the tool that is currently equipped: whether the player has manually equipped their character with a carrot on a stick, an axe or sword (Figure 5.4). Carrying a sword in hand, for instance, visibly shifts the dialogue to the aggressive end of the shape spectrum. This technique is also employed in *The Witcher 3: Wild Hunt* (2015), by CD Projekt RED, where players can enter towns, villages, and encampments with their weapons either sheathed or drawn, which determines whether the AI-controlled inhabitants remain passive or turn hostile (Figure 5.5). The experience is very dramatic because players feel their choice of actions have a genuine effect on characters they randomly encounter.

Figure 5.4 Whether players of *Minecraft* (2011), by Mojang, manually equip their character with a carrot on a stick or a sword pictographically, suggests their intentions and affects the aesthetic possibilities of interaction.

Figure 5.5 Players of *The Witcher 3: Wild Hunt* (2015), by CD Projekt RED, can choose whether to be friendly or aggressive toward the game's virtual inhabitants simply by sheathing or drawing their weapons when entering a town, village, or encampment.

Player-Driven Dialogue

The reason why *Minecraft* and *The Witcher 3: Wild Hunt* are so successful can be partially explained by the expressive scope given to players, which allows them to articulate a wide range of emotions through gameplay actions. More often than not, games are designed to facilitate dialogue within a narrow aesthetic range that constrains players to good or evil roles that remain constant for the entire duration of gameplay.

The "Dark Zone" in *The Division* (2016), by Ubisoft, demonstrates a similar example of player-driven nonverbal dialogue (Figure 5.6) to that of *Minecraft* and *The Witcher 3*. The Dark Zone is a portion of *The Division*'s gameplay map dedicated to player-versus-player gameplay where battles over powerful weaponry and special items lead to high-stakes encounters with rival teams. Surviving an escapade into the Dark Zone necessitates that players enter the area in cooperative teams for mutual support. A standoff occurs whenever a team encounters players outside their group. Assuming a gunfight doesn't immediately break out, both teams must quickly assess each other's skill level (a value visible above each character's head) and the gadgets and weaponry adorning the characters. To display a sign of good intentions, the player's character can express a hands-up gesture of surrender. If the standoff successfully concludes without a fight, ambivalent alliances can be formed with the rival team to clear areas with particularly dangerous mutual enemies. Or friendly players can be added to the player's team via a menu, which switches off the possibility of accidental friendly fire.

The postapocalyptic theme of *The Division*, however, means that alliances can quickly turn to betrayal. The moment that somebody intentionally fires on

Figure 5.6 Players that enter the player-versus-player area in *The Division* (2016), by Ubisoft, can perform actions that allow for positive nonverbal dialogue, such as a peaceful sign of surrender, or a menu for adding new team members.

a human player the gameplay dynamic changes dramatically—causing the individual or team to be flagged as rogue agents (Figure 5.7). A skull icon instantly appears above the miscreants, and every player in the Dark Zone is invited to administer justice for a set period of time. Assuming the rogue agents survive the manhunt, all is forgiven once the timer runs out. In essence, the game enables

Figure 5.7 If a player in the Dark Zone of *The Division* (2016), by Ubisoft, becomes disruptive by intentionally firing on other players, they are instantly flagged as rogue agents on the game's multiplayer map and become open to condemnation by anybody playing nearby.

various forms of dialogue between players but the rogue agent mechanic enforces a code of conduct that is marshalled by the players themselves.

Universal Language

The great thing about dialogue in games is that it promotes a universal form of communication that disregards the player's native language. The set of actions that players are afforded constitute the language unique to each game. Everybody can understand each other within the context set out by the game's infrastructure. Like participants in a dance class, it doesn't matter if everybody speaks a different language as long as they can physically follow the instructor's lead. Actions that are appropriate for *The Division*'s postapocalyptic setting, for instance, will feel completely out of place in a delicate game like *Journey*.

Journey strips away all forms of conventional communication and offers players little more than the ability to jump, chime, draw shapes in the sand, and gesture with movement. This narrow set of expressive possibilities ensures that dialogue between players remains at the game's predefined circular end of the shape spectrum. For instance, *Journey*'s unique approach to online multiplayer gives solitary players the option of partnering with one other traveler at a time. Travelling with a companion is encouraged with a boost to the character's glide ability, which is activated by the simple gesture of close proximity. The players' glowing scarves affectionately wrap around each other for comfort as they progress, to further enhance the sense of serendipitous friendship (Figure 5.8).

It's virtually impossible to perform a negative gesture in *Journey*. The delicate nature of gameplay creates a caring atmosphere that compels experienced players to guide first-timers to hidden locations and resources using musical chimes to

Figure 5.8 The characters in *Journey* (2012), by thatgamecompany, are adorned with scarves that affectionately wrap around their traveling companions—giving a semblance of comfort when the path becomes hazardous.

Figure 5.9 Players of *Journey* (2012), by thatgamecompany, can use musical chimes and draw shapes with their tracks to communicate excitement, and alert each other to interesting locations.

indicate their location (Figure 5.9). The chimes are reminiscent of whales calling to each other across the abyss. Players can also use chimes to communicate excitement, or draw shapes in the snow to show their appreciation. If either player decides to go it alone, they can enact their goodbye wordlessly by moving away from the other at any time.

Scripted Dialogue

The player-driven dialogue that we've examined in *Minecraft*, *The Division*'s multiplayer area, and *Journey* does not adhere to a structure, which means that there is no right or wrong outcome for the nonverbal dialogue that occurs between characters. It's entirely up to players to decide how they express themselves using the language unique to each game. In the context of a scripted narrative, however, dialogue must take on a structure with purpose. The reason for this is that the player is no longer the master of proceedings but a guest who willingly adopts a persona created by the game's scriptwriters. Scripted dialogue presents players with a cast of secondary characters whose roles are already defined in the context of a narrative. These characters must take the conversational reins that shape the player's identity and purpose using various scripted prompts—like a *prompter* who helps theater actors deliver their lines. If the player does not cooperate, the result is usually mission failure or delayed progress. The narrative is allowed to advance and players are rewarded if they perform in line with their appropriated role.

Cutscene Prompts

A hallmark of the *Grand Theft Auto* (*GTA*) franchise, by Rockstar North, is player-driven gameplay. However, each installment in the series also features a scripted narrative woven into the game's open-world environments that players can experience by activating special missions. In contrast to the player-driven dialogue that we also explored in *Minecraft*—which allows players to define their own adventures—these special missions apply a narrative structure that players must adhere to if they wish to progress. The complexity of video game development usually means that characters are often given a single role to perform (be it friend or foe) within such missions, which results in nonverbal dialogue of a singular aesthetic. *GTA: San Andreas* (2004)

CJ, my dog! Whassup? Hey baby, you okay, man?

Figure 5.10 *Grand Theft Auto: San Andreas* (2004), by Rockstar Games, employs noninteractive cutscenes—such as the friendly reunion between CJ and Big Smoke—to establish the narrative context for player interactions once gameplay resumes.

is an exemplary game in this respect because it features a secondary character known as Big Smoke whose aesthetic alignment shifts from ally to enemy—correspondingly causing the nonverbal dialogue between Big Smoke and the playable character to shift from a friendly, circular aesthetic to a triangular conflict (Figure 5.10).

Each scripted mission in *GTA: San Andreas* starts with a noninteractive cutscene, which is the first prompt that shapes the player's shifting relationship with Big Smoke. These cutscenes set the context for the player's actions once gameplay resumes and the dialogue shifts to actions, not words. During gameplay players actively experience their relationship with Big Smoke through various in-game prompts that include scripted banter, body language, a player-dependent health gauge, and Big Smoke's designated shooting targets.

Gameplay Prompts

For instance, a mission in *GTA: San Andreas* called "Just Business" sees the player and Big Smoke fighting side-by-side against a common enemy (Figure 5.11). The two characters exchange scripted banter as they progress, which sets the mood and provides players with useful clues on how to proceed through the level. A gauge located in the upper-middle of the frame displays Big Smoke's health, which instructs players to protect their comrade or face mission failure should the gauge be depleted by enemy fire.

By the game's end Big Smoke has betrayed his fellow gang members and the playable character, CJ—forcing a climatic faceoff in a bout of last man standing (Figure 5.12). For the final mission titled "End of the Line," the game's designers have adjusted Big Smoke's underlying attributes to make him a more formidable enemy. Simply increasing his health, stamina, and shooting accuracy settings

Figure 5.11 When Big Smoke from *Grand Theft Auto: San Andreas* (2004), by Rockstar Games, is an ally, he fights alongside the player who is responsible for Big Smoke's survival via a health gauge positioned in top-middle of the frame.

Figure 5.12 When Big Smoke betrays the playable character his programmed behavior becomes confrontational, and the player is tasked with depleting Big Smoke's health gauge to complete the story.

is usually too subtle for players to perceive, so a bulletproof vest worn by Big Smoke visually accounts for his increased resilience to gunshots and heavier weaponry conveys his increased shooting abilities. To finish the final mission, players must deplete Big Smoke's health gauge before their own character runs out of health, which is in stark contrast to the earlier mission when players were tasked with the opposite—of ensuring that Big Smoke's health gauge sustained as little damage as possible.

Branching Narratives

Player-driven and scripted dialogue can coexist in the same game world but the approaches to interaction tend to be kept separate due to present limitations in artificial intelligence. A game that combines both narrative forms—a scripted story that allows total player freedom—would require an intelligent system that adapts to the player's choices on the fly. Such artificial intelligence would have to be as smart as a human *gamemaster* in a traditional role-playing game—able to author and direct a story that makes dramatic sense, while refereeing and managing the game's rules so that gameplay and story can organically evolve in unison. The current alternative is to give players a choice but limit their options to key moments in the narrative. This is nonetheless a work-intensive solution for game developers because the outcome of each *narrative branch*—the point at which a player chooses to follow plot X or Y—must be manually crafted even if players never choose to experience all possibilities.

An exponentially branching structure (Figure 5.13b) is therefore clearly impractical in most cases due to the number of assets that must be generated for each outcome. As a result, most games with a scripted narrative stick to one linear plot (Figure 5.13a) because orchestrating game design, artwork, animations, and audio is difficult and expensive enough without worrying about player choice. A midway solution is to use a parallel structure (Figure 5.13c). Games with a parallel structure rely on skillful scriptwriting to give the illusion of player freedom while periodically reconvening the parallel plots at important junctures—illustrated as *nodes*—to ensure the total amount of story content remains manageable. This usually means that a game's levels only have one entrance and one exit, but the pathways in-between will differ depending on player choices. Concluding the narrative with multiple endings can further heighten the illusion of player-freedom. The reduced set of narrative options compared to exponentially branching narratives nonetheless creates a satisfactory sense of narrative ownership for players.

The illustrations in Figure 5.13 can be used as shorthand notation when discussing story and dialogue: the nodes designating important decision points can be indicated with primary shapes, and the branches between each node representing various pathways can likewise be shaped using curved, straight, or angular lines.

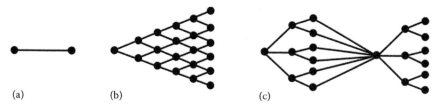

(a)   (b)   (c)

Figure 5.13 (a) A linear narrative with a single plot; (b) an exponentially branching structure; and (c) a parallel structure that periodically reconvenes.

Multiple-Choice Dialogue

Despite the inherent technical challenges of scripting interactive stories, developers have successfully enabled players to make scripted narratives feel like their own via multiple-choice dialogue during semi-interactive cutscenes. One such game is *The Walking Dead* series by Telltale Games. Players loading an episode from the series are presented with the following statement: "This game series adapts to the choices you make. The story is tailored by how you play." The series periodically confronts players with difficult decisions that determine the dynamics within their group of survivors who are clambering to stay alive in the midst of a zombie apocalypse (Figure 5.14). Their options can be generalized as agreeable (circle), neutral (square), or aggravating (triangle)—although choices are often ambiguous because siding with one character may inadvertently split relations with another. Which option players ultimately choose affects how other characters respond to their playable character and consequences may not become apparent until several hours of subsequent gameplay have elapsed.

The concept of enabling morally ambiguous choices may sound redundant to non-video game players, since such outcomes are an inherent aspect of real life. However, they are less common in video games simply due to the technical obstacles concerning scripted narratives discussed earlier. To put the workload into context, a big-budget game like *The Witcher 3: Wild Hunt* (2015) by CD Projekt RED, features around 450,000 voice-acted words—roughly equivalent to four books—that had to be managed for consistency and continuity. Players are generally forgiving if animations are rudimentary, but voice acting and narrative must be of the highest quality.

Figure 5.14 *The Walking Dead* video game series (2012), by Telltale Games, confronts players with difficult decisions that threaten to divide the group of survivors—such as whether to side with Christa and let her injured boyfriend rest, search for Chuck, or agree with Kenny and head to the river in search of an escape boat.

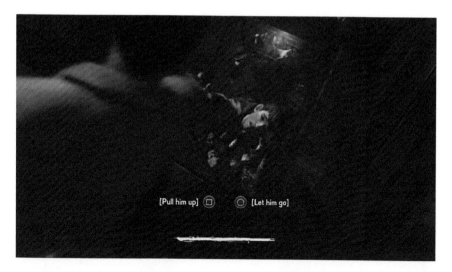

Figure 5.15 The above moment in *The Walking Dead: Episode 4* (2012) by Telltale Games, when players must decide whether to permit the hapless character, Ben, to sacrifice himself or attempt a rescue in the face of advancing zombies is intensified with polarizing options that must be selected within a time limit.

Although interactivity during multiple-choice dialogue involves the simple tap of a button that corresponds to the player's choice, Telltale Games uses various techniques to vary aesthetic intensity. For instance, a countdown that resembles a burning dynamite fuse indicates the time remaining for players to make a choice. A subtler technique is to present players with two options, which creates a polarizing effect that feels tenser than when three or four options are available (Figure 5.15).

Semi-interactive cutscenes are currently the preferred method to present players with meaningful choices but this certainly is not the definitive approach, since branching decisions can be offered to players during gameplay. The key concern is to ensure that players are aware of the moment's significance, which is easier to orchestrate with a cutscene that brings all the action to a momentous focal point.

Exposition

Games can also take a one-sided approach to communication with players through written notes, diary entries, and letters. Such narrative devices should be used sparingly because players generally wish to get on with interactivity. It's not that players don't enjoy reading—rather that they prefer their games to be about gameplay. However, this entirely depends on the pace and style of the game in question. Written narrative information may be a necessity for development budget reasons or a welcome story layer for players who enjoy delving into every aspect of a plot. *Gone Home* (2013), by The Fullbright Company, prominently features written memos to communicate much of the story. Certain memos in *Gone Home* are accompanied by a voice-acted recording, which makes them more effective at conveying plot details than pure written text because players can passively experience the content without disruption to gameplay. When text is used by itself to convey dialogue between characters it is often presented in a convenient format that resembles an e-mail conversation thread consisting of written paragraphs from alternating contributors. To ensure that each memo makes a quick visual impression—whether or not it is read—the game's developers varied the designs of each page and handwriting to visually summarize the content's sentiment as seen in Figure 5.16.

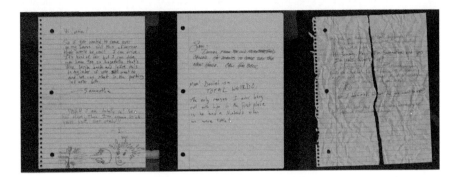

Figure 5.16 From left to right: a dialogue between the sweethearts of *Gone Home* (2013), by The Fullbright Company, is adorned with goofy drawings; the mother's request is written with clear handwriting that is contrasted by the daughter's childish script, and the torn and crumpled paper leaves no doubt about the protagonist's feelings toward the obnoxious neighbor.

Figure 5.17 The veiled statues located throughout *Bloodborne* (2015), by FromSoftware, give context to the city of Yharnam and hint at a backstory that inquisitive players can piece together as they proceed.

Environment Storytelling

Yet another approach to convey narrative is through environment storytelling. For instance, the environments and secondary characters of *Bloodborne* (2015), by FromSoftware, suggest an especially rich lore that forms the backstory of the game (Figure 5.17). Players are encouraged to piece together the narrative's backstory through environmental clues that permeate the city of Yharnam in which the game takes place. Players of *Bloodborne* will undoubtedly be intrigued by the significance of Provost Willem's blindfold, Cloaked Beast Patient monsters, and the veiled statues scattered around the decrepit world of Yharnam—all of which allude to a backstory concerning sight. Such content adds authenticity to the game world, which players can voluntarily investigate should they wish.

Language Training

Because gameplay is a form of nonverbal communication, it is important to teach players the grammar particular to each language in comfortable stages—rather than all at once. In a game like *Journey*, the elegantly simple controls mean that nearly every expressive action is available to players from the outset. Games with a larger expressive *vocabulary* must introduce character abilities gradually so as not to overwhelm players with too much information. Nintendo's certified classic, *The Legend of Zelda: Ocarina of Time* (1998), is a superb reference for structuring the introduction and assimilation of large amounts of character abilities. We can get an idea of the player's expressive scope in *Ocarina of Time* just by looking at the range of equipable items in the inventory menus in Figure 5.18, which feature items essential to overcoming the game's many dungeon puzzles.

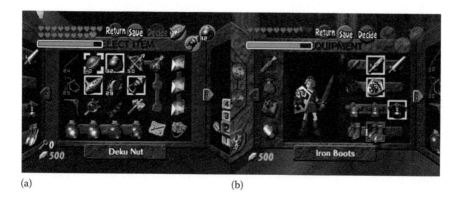

(a)   (b)

Figure 5.18 The Select Item menu (a) and Equipment menu (b) in *The Legend of Zelda: Ocarina of Time* (1998), by Nintendo, are initially empty but gradually fill up with items as the character progresses through the game—unlocking further items and locations with each new ability.

Figure 5.19 The entrance to Dodongo's Cavern in *The Legend of Zelda: Ocarina of Time* (1998), by Nintendo, clearly communicates the dungeon's expressive theme by tasking players with plucking a bomb from the bomb flower and throwing it at the cracked dungeon entrance located in the immediate vicinity.

Language Pacing

Ocarina of Time's playable character, Link, starts out with a limited set of basic abilities that include running, rolling, jumping, and climbing. Core gameplay items are gradually added to Link's initial repertoire of moves at predetermined points across the game's 30 hours of gameplay. Whenever a new item is unlocked, players are subsequently directed to a dungeon containing puzzles specifically designed to test the player's skills with that particular item. For instance, the puzzles in "Dodongo's Cavern" are solved using increasingly elaborate solutions using the newly acquired bomb item (Figure 5.19). The player's progress through the dungeon culminates in an enemy boss fight with King Dodongo himself, who is especially susceptible to bomb attacks, while the "Inside Jabu-Jabu's Belly" dungeon forces players to utilize the boomerang before testing their mastery of the weapon against the dungeon boss, Bio-electric Anenome Barinade. You can think of each dungeon as a school semester—designed to test the player's command of the game's language—and the end-of-level boss as the final exam. Players of *Ocarina of Time* "graduate" once they overcome the inevitable final boss, Ganon, whose alternating attacks require that players combine all the abilities they've learned in the lead-up to the climactic encounter. Level designer Pete Ellis—who has worked on games like *Killzone Shadow Fall* (2013), by Guerrilla Games—describes the player's education process as consisting of three stages: exposition, validation, and challenge:

> This is that you show the player the thing you will be teaching them, you let them experience it and use the mechanic themselves in a safe area, and then you give them a challenge to prove they understand how to use it.

Dialogue Notation

The shorthand notation for dialogue is a simple word balloon containing primary shapes or text descriptions. The shape of the word balloon itself can also be modulated to suggest the dialogue's aesthetic theme using designs familiar to readers of comics.

Barrier to Recommencing Play

A word of caution to developers regarding games that offer players a large number of abilities. Gradually introducing new skills works fine if players frequently return to the game and make regular progress. However, players may sometimes refrain from playing for long periods, which makes it increasingly daunting to start-up the game and resume where they left off. Just the notion of having to relearn all the skills that players have accumulated in previous gaming sessions leads many to give up altogether! A contingency should therefore be considered to refresh the skills of returning players for long games that have a large number of expressive possibilities.

Summary

From the above examples we can see that dialogue comes in many forms but video gaming's strength is in nonverbal dialogue. The dialogue unique to each game is like a language that must be gradually learned if players are to successfully interact with the game world. Character classes and skills are the values that drive character behavior. Games offer richer expressive possibilities if they allow players to personalize classes and skills as well as the appearance of their playable character.

Now that we've examined five elements of dynamic composition that occur on-screen—character shapes and poses, lines of movement, environment shapes, pathways, and dialogue—we can consider the aesthetic qualities of framing these elements with a camera as well as methods for directing the player's gaze to important objects and events. We will also explore the emotional effects of manipulating the in-game camera to affect the player's sense of well-being.

 Framing

Framing concerns the manner in which in-game action is viewed within the bounds of the picture frame—whether the frame is a monitor, mobile phone, virtual reality headset, or any other digital screen. Our principal considerations for framing are camera angles, proximity to the playable character, and directing the player's gaze.

The Camera's Influence on Emotions and Gameplay

A general rule is that players experience a more intimate connection with their playable character when the camera is positioned up-close. The screenshots below include a *first-person*, or point-of-view, camera (Figure 6.1a), and a *close-up* camera (Figure 6.1b). A gameplay close-up is different to a film close-up because it usually frames the back of the playable character's head, since it must face the direction of action in line with the player's gaze. The synchronization of perspectives creates a visceral experience because in-game events appear to be directed straight at the player. This is especially true of the first-person view, which hides all but the arms of the in-game figure—thus perfectly aligning the player's gaze with that of their in-game character. For close-ups, playable characters are usually positioned off to one side so as not to disturb the player's view of the environment.

Framing the action using a *mid-shot* (Figure 6.2a) or *long-shot* (Figure 6.2b) shifts the experience away from the player's first-person perspective to focus on the playable character, whose shape and animations can be clearly seen within the picture frame. The experience feels more intimate the closer a camera is positioned to the playable character.

(a)   (b)

Figure 6.1 (a) *Portal 2* (2011) by Valve Corporation. (b) *Gears of War 3* (2011) by Epic Games. First-person and close-up cameras create a heightened sense of player-character empathy because the player's perspective aligns with that of the playable character.

(a)   (b)

Figure 6.2 (a) *Gears of War 3* (2011) by Epic Games. (b) *Metal Gear Solid V: The Phantom Pain* (2015) by Kojima Productions. Mid-shots and long-shots afford players a clearer view of the playing field and the playable character's expressive shapes and animations.

Last, we have *extreme long-shots* (Figure 6.3), where visual prominence is given to the entire playing field. Extreme long-shots create a sense of detachment from in-game characters and are most often used for strategy games that require a bird's-eye view of the environment so that players can tactically respond to events. The sense of detachment can also be used to emphasize a sense of loneliness.

A cut between mid-shots and close-ups is often used in games like the *Assassin's Creed*, and *Batman Arkham* series. During combat, a mid-shot (Figure 6.4a) is used to give players a broad overview of battle and approaching enemies. For the takedown of an enemy, the camera cuts to a noninteractive close-up (Figure 6.4b), which captures the brutal details of knocks and punches.

It's important to note that terms like close-up and long-shot originate from photography and cinema, which are mediums that can freely switch between shot types due to their lack of interactivity. Video games do not have the same freedom because they involve such a complex system of interactions that the camera set-up must be optimized for the player's command of gameplay, lest the experience

Figure 6.3 Extreme long-shots are commonly used in strategic games like *Heroes of the Storm* (2015), by Blizzard Entertainment, to provide players with a commanding view of the playing field—although long-shots can equally be used for aesthetic effect.

becomes too confusing or breaks altogether. The technical overhead is simply too high to ensure that a game remains playable irrespective of how it's framed. This is the reason why each shot type is usually associated with a particular genre of gaming, as opposed to being a fluid cinematic device. Games like *Fahrenheit* (2005) and *Valiant Hearts: The Great War* (2014) offer solutions to this dilemma using comic book-style nested frames, and highlight the aesthetic value to be gained from fluid shifts between close-ups, mid-shots, long-shots, and extreme long-shots during gameplay (see Chapter 11, Dual Perspectives with Nested Frames section).

Creating Layers of Emotions with Camera Angles

Low-angle, *mid-angle*, and *high-angle* shots add a second layer of aesthetic influence when framing in-game action—as demonstrated by *Uncharted 4: A Thief's End* (Figure 6.5). Low-angles make subjects look heroic, dominant, and strong; mid-angles place the subject on a neutral, equal level with their surroundings; and high-angles diminish the subject, which appears small when viewed from above. This latter effect is often used in horror games to amplify feelings of trepidation by having players descend a staircase because it spatially directs players toward a vulnerable or submissive position—which can be underscored with music that has a descending melodic theme. Conversely, themes of heroism and elation can be heightened by having players ascend a staircase that elevates them to a dominant vantage point. Of course, both concepts can be subverted to counter player expectations.

For each vantage point, it is important to identify the primary subject of the shot. In most narrative-driven video games, players control the main protagonist who faces away from the camera and becomes somewhat peripheral because the

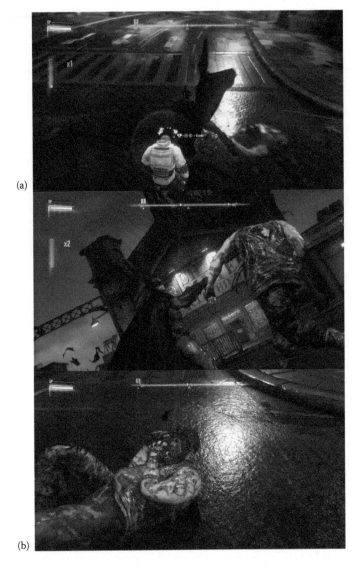

(a)

(b)

Figure 6.4 A dynamic camera is used in *Batman: Arkham Knight* (2015), by Rocksteady Studios, during fight sequences to give players a tactical long-shot during battle (a), and a visceral close-up (b) for enemy takedowns.

player's attention is turned to obstacles in the environment (Figure 6.6). This also serves to help the player identify with the on-screen character. Consequently, the main subjects within the frame are often secondary characters. Therefore, it's the enemies in Figure 6.5 who are the main subject and not the playable character.

If Nathan Drake—the main protagonist of *Uncharted 4: A Thief's End*—suddenly becomes the subject during gameplay or a cutscene, then a high-angle

Figure 6.5 (a–c) Low-angle, mid-angle, and high-angle shots in *Uncharted 4: A Thief's End* (2016), by Naughty Dog, dynamically affect the player's sense of empowerment in relation to enemies and the environment.

shot will make him look vulnerable (Figure 6.7), in contrast to Figure 6.5c in which the subjects are Nathan's enemies so a high-angle shot emphasizes his dominance. In short: the dominant individual is the person (or creature) on top. The framing concepts of low-, mid-, and high-angles reflect real-life interactions between people in conversation, such as: lowering your gaze in submission, or lifting your head to look down your nose at somebody.

Replay

Uncharted 4: A Thief's End (2016), by Naughty Dog
Publisher: Sony Computer Entertainment

   Play through your favorite video game featuring parkour-style game-play—such as *Batman: Arkham Knight* (2015), *Assassin's Creed: Syndicate* (2015), or *Uncharted 4: A Thief's End* (2016). Pay particular attention to your sense of well-being when at ground level versus up on the rooftops or high vantage points. Do enemies appear more or less threatening when you approach them from above or below?

Figure 6.6 This edited screenshot from *Uncharted 4: A Thief's End* (2016), by Naughty Dog, features a blur effect to illustrate the player's visual impression of gameplay, which casts the playable character to the periphery and focuses attention on obstacles and user interface information.

Player-Controlled Camera Angles

Unlike close-ups, medium-shots, and long-shots—which cannot be switched freely due to gameplay considerations—camera angles in 3D games tend to be under player control. This means that players can dynamically pivot the in-game camera to frame the action according to their gameplay needs. *Mass Effect 3*'s senior designer, Dave Feltham, and the team at BioWare skillfully designed the "Cure the Genophage" level (Figure 6.8) to indirectly motivate players to tilt the in-game camera between a low- and mid-angle for aesthetic effect. In the opening section of the level, the Reaper enemy and its red laser are seen from a low vantage point, which requires players to angle the camera upward—thus increasing the Reaper's

Figure 6.7 In the above cutscene from *Uncharted 4: A Thief's End* (2016), by Naughty Dog, Nathan Drake is the main subject so a high-angle shot makes him appear vulnerable.

visual dominance (Figure 6.8a). By the level's end, the character has run up a series of steps (Figure 6.8b) to find herself on equal ground with the Reaper (Figure 6.8c), which has the effect of increasing the player's sense of empowerment. Because camera angles have such a powerful affect on the player's sense of well-being, it is important to use environment design to encourage players to explore the environment from various vantage points in service of the narrative.

The distribution of secondary characters and props in the environment can additionally prompt players to adjust the camera for aesthetic effect. For instance, channeling enemies down a linear path results in players centering the camera on one area of the environment—as in Figure 6.9a from *Uncharted 4: A Thief's End*. While the sporadic placement of enemies in an exposed area (Figure 6.9b) forces players to chaotically rotate the camera in an attempt to locate the origins of bullet tracers. The same technique can be used to distribute important props, such as switches to doorways, so that players experience an increase in tension if the switch and the doorway cannot be framed from one perspective.

Inducing Discomfort with Canted Camera Angles

A camera technique that is underused in games is the *canted-angle* (or Dutch-angle), which creates a dynamic effect and can also communicate the playable character's distress or discomfort. Empathy for the character's state of mind is heightened because the tilted frame also puts players off-balance. An instance of camera tilt is evidenced during combat in *Prince of Persia* (2008), by Ubisoft, where the tilt happens momentarily so that players may not even notice the visual imbalance that is certain to create a sense of unease (Figure 6.10). You'll find

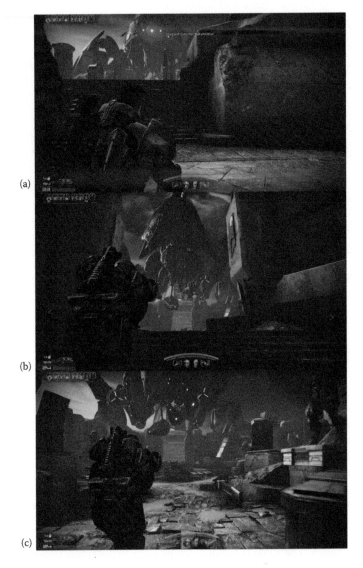

(a)

(b)

(c)

Figure 6.8 (a–c) Players are encouraged to adjust the camera from a low- to mid-angle as they ascend a series of steps to reach equal ground with the enemy during the "Cure the Genophage" level in *Mass Effect 3* (2012), by BioWare.

a similar application of canted cameras in *Rise of the Tomb Raider* (2015), by Crystal Dynamic, whenever Lara Croft performs leaps across large gaps.

Alternatively, the environment can be titled instead of the camera to heighten tension. Players experience this disorientating affect in the escape sequence from *Halo 4* (2012), by 343 Industries, in which the ground plane is tilted to create a canted effect while the camera's angle remains fixed (Figure 6.11).

(a)   (b)

Figure 6.9 Level design that channels gameplay down a single corridor (a) can be contrasted with sporadic placement of secondary characters in an open area (b) to elicit focused or searching camera movements, respectively—such as in these examples from *Uncharted 4: A Thief's End* (2016), by Naughty Dog.

Figure 6.10 The gameplay camera in *Prince of Persia* (2008), by Ubisoft, tilts momentarily when players attack important enemies, which creates dramatic tension through visual imbalance.

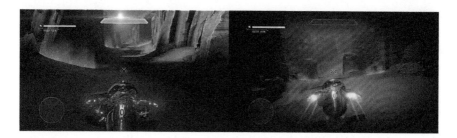

Figure 6.11 The above gameplay sequence from *Halo 4* (2012), by 343 Industries, uses a tilted environment to create the same effect as a canted camera angle.

Directing the Player's Gaze

There will be many instances when designers wish to draw the player's attention to important story events during gameplay. This can be a tricky task in 3D environments where players often have full control of the camera. Placing a *frame-within-a-frame* and *signposting* are highly effective ways to direct a player's gaze.

Doorways are the most common method to create a frame-within-a-frame. The visual device narrows the player's field of view in an otherwise open environment. Doorways are used repeatedly in games like the *Halo* series (Figure 6.12) in combination with events that are automatically activated just as the player approaches, which together provide an instant overview of enemy formations and incoming drop ships up ahead. Alternatively, a vignette formed of high contrast objects in the environment (Figure 6.13) can be employed to achieve the same effect as a doorway.

Centering

Additionally, *centering* important objects within the frame ensures that they command visual dominance, such as the bright pillar in the background of Figure 6.13. Similarly, consider the central placement of the playable character in third-person games and side-scrollers. If the protagonists in games like the *Uncharted* series were positioned off to one side, and not center of frame, they would no longer command visual importance—although such an effect can have a useful narrative or compositional function.

Figure 6.12 *Halo 4* (2012), by 343 Industries, makes excellent use of doorways and architecture to create a frame-within-a-frame that channels the player's gaze toward important events in the environment.

Figure 6.13 The monolithic white structure in the background of this environment from *Halo 4* (2012), by 343 Industries, commands visual attention because of its central placement and the vignette formed by the surrounding architecture.

Signposting

Signposting (Figure 6.14) is the method of using lines and shapes embedded in the environment to create a visual breadcrumb trail in much the same way as the classical composition techniques explored in *Drawing Basics and Video Game Art: Classic to Cutting-Edge Art Techniques for Winning Game Design* (Watson-Guptill 2012). Using frame-within-a-frame or signposting makes gameplay feel significantly more immersive because players feel that they are finding their own way—as opposed to being directed via noninteractive cutscenes, prompts in the user interface, or dialogue.

Contrast

Directing the player's gaze can also be achieved through contrasting visual elements. The technique works by drawing the player's gaze to the inverse of what is typical for a particular environment. For instance, a triangular object in an environment predominantly composed of circular shapes will be perceived as a visual exclamation mark. A whole range of contrasting visual elements can be used for this technique, including: animation, shapes, color, value, scale, density of objects, regularity, and so forth.

Contrast of Speed and Animation

For instance, chase missions in the *Assassin's Creed* series demonstrate how contrasting animations can be used to direct the player's gaze (Figure 6.15). During the "Cruel Caricature" side mission in *Assassin's Creed: Syndicate* (2015), the player is tasked with chasing a carriage that is driven erratically and significantly faster than the general traffic—making it easy to track the object of pursuit.

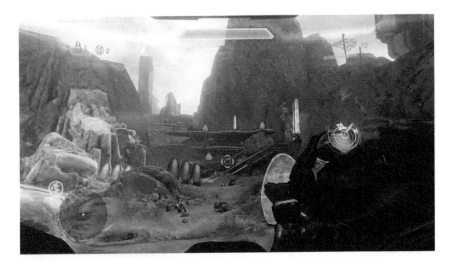

Figure 6.14 Signposting can be complimented by a considered placement of prominent objects—such as in this example from *Halo 4*, by 343 Industries, in which the lines of receding architectural platforms and glowing shields clearly orientate players towards their objective.

Figure 6.15 A contrast of speed is used to direct the player's gaze to the most erratic and fastest moving carriage during chase missions in *Assassin's Creed: Syndicate* (2015), by Ubisoft.

Contrast of Color

The "Runner Vision" feature in *Mirror's Edge* highlights paths and escape routes with vibrant red and orange hues, which are coded to communicate surfaces that are helpful for navigating the environment (Figure 6.16). These vibrantly colored elements are easy for players to discern due to their contrast with the stark whiteness of the game's cityscape.

Figure 6.16 *Mirror's Edge* (2008), by DICE, employs vibrant red and orange hues to direct the player's gaze toward important escape routes.

The Importance of Medium Values

The opening desert environment in *Journey* is a particularly great example of using several contrasting visual elements to direct the player's gaze. The rolling sand dunes serve as a medium value canvas upon which important elements can be discerned due to their high contrast values, shape, scale, and density. For instance, the bright mountaintop in Figure 6.17 commands attention against the medium-value landscape; rectangular and angular shapes contrast the rounded forms of the dunes; and the clustering of dark tombstones creates a visual noise that contrasts larger, flat shapes. Designers are advised to exercise restraint by using medium values for the majority of visual and interactive elements, so that the strongest contrasts can be reserved for important story elements.

Face-to-Face Contact

As with real-life interactions with people, we should not forget that seeing the playable character's face is an effective way to establish an emotional connection. Side-scrollers like Media Molecule's *LittleBigPlanet 3* (2014) give players continued opportunities to experience the facial expressions of the series' protagonist (Figure 6.18). Nesting characters within the frame is another solution to bring players face-to-face with secondary characters irrespective of where the player is currently directing his or her attention within the environment. Such a technique is best suited for situations where the dramatic fourth wall can be broken. For instance, *Tearaway: Unfolded* (2015) by Media Molecule, is one such example of using nested characters to make players feel a part of the game world (Figure 6.19).

Figure 6.17 The opening landscape in *Journey* (2012), by thatgamecompany, is predominantly composed of medium values and simple large shapes, which help draw the player's gaze to objects of importance that are rendered with extreme light and dark values.

Figure 6.18 Side-scrollers like *LittleBigPlanet 3* (2014), by Media Molecule, give players a continued sideview of the game's endearing playable character, whose face would otherwise be turned away with a first- or third-person camera.

Figure 6.19 *Tearaway: Unfolded* (2015), by Media Molecule, uses nested characters silhouetted against the in-game environment to bring players face-to-face with secondary characters.

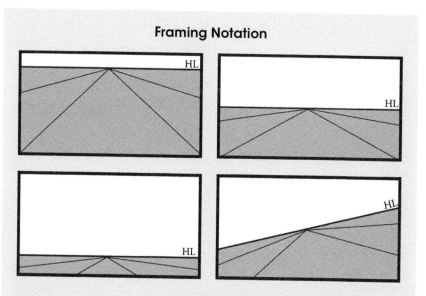

The notation for framing is an empty rectangle with a horizontal line marked "HL." The area above the horizon line represents the sky, and the area below represents the ground plane, which can be indicated with perspective guidelines or horizontal shading.

Summary

The above examples highlight important considerations for framing a game's action—including identification of the subject within the frame, camera proximity to the subject, camera angles, and techniques for drawing the player's gaze to important information. Low camera angles tend to create a sense of vulnerability because of the insect-like perspective makes the player perceive that everything in the environment appears bigger and imposing. Mid-angles place the character on an equal level in the environment. And high-angles create a sense of empowerment because of the player's dominant, bird's-eye perspective of the surroundings. Games that prompt players to frame in-game events using all three angles—low-, mid-, and high-angles—will undoubtedly have a richer aesthetic scope than games with a single-angle setup. By using the various methods to direct the viewer's gaze—frame-within-a-frame, centering, signposting, and contrasting visual elements—we can ensure that players in 3D environments will always be looking in the right direction at precisely the right time when special events occur. What unites all the examples for directing the player's gaze is that the environments are overall visually neutral, allowing designers to judiciously use extreme contrasts to emphasize points of interest.

The next chapter shifts away from the visual senses to explore our sense of sound in the context of video game audio. Although, as we'll find, music and sound effects have an interesting connection to visual art and interaction that will help us to find aesthetic relationships to the shape spectrum.

7 Audio

Video games would only deliver a fraction of their immersive potential without the support of audio. Audio alone can transform the aesthetic experience of gameplay by providing an ambient atmosphere for the player's actions. Audio is a term that covers two principle categories in the context of games: music and sound effects. Music and sound effects are applied to both interactive and non-interactive moments of a video game experience that begins the instant the game is switched on and a start menu is loaded. This chapter, however, focuses on audio that supports gameplay—when players are in control of a video game character.

Waves, Dancing, and Gameplay

Audio is unquestionably a nonvisual medium, which makes it difficult to imagine how it fits with the visual-based shape spectrum. When considering audio we must simplify our task of translating visual-based aesthetic concepts to nonvisual sound by exploring sound's relationships to visual phenomena. The most apt example is illustrated by waves at sea because of their physical relationship to acoustics and the study of sound waves. You'll have to close your eyes and imagine the soundscape for each state: the sound of rolling waves that reference the harmonious and positive energy of the circle (Figure 7.1a); a serene and quiet sea that references the stable square (Figure 7.1b); and the clashing, discordant sounds of storm waves (Figure 7.1c).

Another example of visual phenomena derived from sound—and one that directly benefits our investigation of audio and gameplay—is the relationship between music and dancing. This is because dancing is a physical interpretation of music—turning something that is intangible and making it tangible. Music has

(a)   (b)   (c)

Figure 7.1 Sea conditions aptly illustrate how the aesthetic concepts of visual shapes relate to the nonvisual realm of sound: the acoustics of rolling waves reference the circle (a), the hushed sounds of calm waters reference the square (b), and clashing storm waves reference the triangle (c).

such a primal influence on us that it can trigger and choreograph physical activity on a subconscious level. For instance, we've all had the experience of listening to a song and realizing that our feet have been tapping its rhythm without our full awareness. When we dance our whole body becomes instinctively engaged in the act of translating sound into form and movement (although some people are more naturally gifted than others!).

The principal components of music that pull on our kinesthetic strings when we dance are *tone, rhythm and tempo,* and *melody.* Understanding how these three components choreograph physical activity has obvious connotations for gameplay, where player gestures are central to the aesthetic experience of narrative. The concept of musical choreography can only be used loosely in the context of gameplay because the player's priorities are to respond to in-game events that may occur outside of the music's structure (aside from the genre of rhythm-action games that are explicitly designed to synchronize player inputs with music). Therefore, music accompanying gameplay serves to cue players to an appropriate mode of activity. The player's gestures represent an asynchronous interpretation of music that is strongly influenced by the aesthetics of tone, rhythm and tempo, and melody but not coordinated with the same precision as in dance.

Tone

Our definition of tone in music is linked to intonation in speech. The tone of a musical sound can be modulated to express a wide range of aesthetics by varying its duration, pitch, loudness, and textural quality (*timbre*)—just as words can be spoken with a happy, serious, or aggressive tone. When considering the overall tonality of a composition, composers also consider the musical harmonies (chords) and scale of notes upon which the music will be set—such as *major* or *minor* keys—which can cast a positive or negative mood over the entire piece. This relatable concept for tone that links music with speech is synonymous with our shape spectrum, which enables us to use primary shapes as descriptors for the aesthetics of tone. Depending on the context, tones with a high pitch and warm and bright texture (such as a flute) can be described as circular; tones with long duration, low pitch, and dull texture (a bass clarinet) align with the neutral square; and loud tones with a short duration and metallic texture (crash cymbals) can be described as triangular. This is not a conventional frame of reference in music but adapting our artistic sensitivity for visual shapes to sounds allows us to unite all the various disciplines involved in game design under the same dynamic composition framework.

Tone and Player Gestures

The original *Super Mario Bros.* (1985), by Nintendo, defined many game design conventions that are widely used to this day. The game's music—created by video game composer and sound director, Koji Kondo—plays an equal role in helping us understand the aesthetics of tone in the context of primary shapes. *Super Mario Bros.* features three tones to describe three distinct portions of gameplay. The opening for each level starts in the "Overworld" (Figure 7.2a), which is the environment associated with Mario. The tonal quality for the Overworld theme can be described using the same keywords that were used to describe Mario's iconic circular design in Chapter 1 (despite the discrepancy in graphical resolution): dynamic, youthful, and positive. These themes consequently contribute to the player's mood and the manner in which they tap and tilt buttons on the game controller. The circular tones of the Overworld theme become steadier, lengthier, and square when players reach the end-of-level flagpole (Figure 7.2b) and are rewarded with triumphant sounding fanfare. The pitch and textural quality of

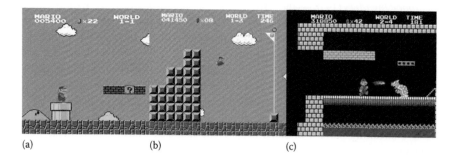

(a)   (b)   (c)

Figure 7.2 *Super Mario Bros.* (1985), by Nintendo, uses a range of positive, triumphant, and threatening tones to musically distinguish (a) Mario's Overworld environment, (b) the end-of-level flagpole, and (c) Bowser's castle, respectively.

tones that greet Mario when players enter the castle of his archenemy, Bowser (Figure 7.2c), have a threatening and triangular quality that contrasts the circular Overworld theme—likewise influencing the player's sense of well-being and physical gestures.

Musical Themes

Super Mario Bros. demonstrates that tone alone can serve as a *leitmotif*, which is a musical phrase (which can be harmonic, rhythmic, melodic, etc.) that is consistently associated with a character, situation, or idea. As gameplay switches between aesthetic concepts, leitmotifs are used to synaesthetically amplify the player's sense of well-being and affect the aesthetic quality of their gestures—whether they tap softly, firmly, or aggressively on the game controller. The principal components of music never act independently of each other so we must also consider how rhythm and tempo, and melody work together with tone to affect player gestures.

Rhythm and Tempo

Hearing is the second of the five senses that we develop—occurring as early as 20 weeks into pregnancy when the auditory system of a fetus becomes functional. This early development of hearing may explain our association of rhythm and tempo with heartbeats and footsteps, which are among the first sounds that are experienced in the womb. A drum beat or bass usually indicates rhythm and has the strongest influence on the structure and frequency of a dancer's steps—much like a musician's metronome. In gameplay terms, rhythm emphasizes movement in the horizontal axes and makes the music feel grounded. Its principal function is to underscore the stride of a playable character (such as walking, skipping, running, or stumbling). Video game composers also use rhythm to encourage varied tempos of player gestures—compelling players to move and perform actions at a rate that loosely matches the beat count. Conversely, stylized pauses (*rests*) within a rhythmic pattern can be employed to induce players to make frequent stops during gameplay.

Space Invaders (1978)—the retro arcade classic by Tomohiro Nishikado—was the first video game to feature a continuous background soundtrack composed of a simple sequence of looping bass notes that were linked to the speed and proximity of the advancing alien army (Figure 7.3). As the aliens converge on the player's position, the steady beat gradually increases in tempo—matching the player's increasing heart rate and activity brought on by the escalating effort to survive.

Similarly, when players descend to *Super Mario Bros.'* "Underworld" (Figure 7.4) via a green pipe, the rhythmic theme of the secret environment suggests a sneaking pattern of steps despite the fact that Mario's movements and gameplay abilities remain unchanged. Notice how the suspenseful pause in rhythm—in the notation accompanying Figure 7.4—occurs in-between three closely packed sets of notes (or implied character steps) that are rhythmically akin to a creeping burglar in search of hidden coins.

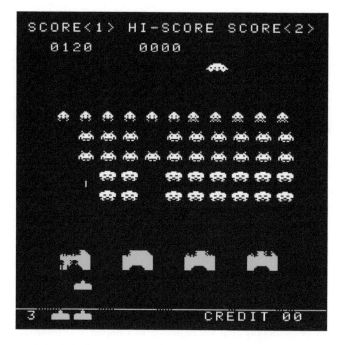

Figure 7.3 *Space Invaders* (1978), by Tomohiro Nishikado, features a steady background rhythm that increases in frequency as the advancing army of aliens approaches the player-controlled laser canon at the bottom of the screen.

Figure 7.4 A fragment from the Underworld theme from *Super Mario Bros.* (1985), by Nintendo, illustrates how rhythm can imply a sneaking pattern of steps even if the playable character's animations remain at the default running pace (music transcribed by BLUESCD).

Also consider how the pace of gameplay is reflected in the rhythm of the original soundtracks (OST) for *Animal Crossing: New Leaf* (2012) (Figure 7.5a) and *Vanquish* (Figure 7.5b). *Animal Crossing: New Leaf* has a soundtrack that dynamically changes according to the player's real-world time. The music at 12PM features a rhythm and tempo that is among the more upbeat tunes in the 24-hour cycle, while the tempo at 7AM is relatively slower and features more pauses that

(a)   (b)

Figure 7.5 (a) The original soundtrack for *Animal Crossing: New Leaf* (2012), by Nintendo, is slow-paced and filled with rhythmic pauses that inspire players to stop and reflect on the game's visually rich and friendly environment. (b) The dense mechanical rhythm of music in *Vanquish* (2010), by PlatinumGames, induces a frenzied tempo and frequency of player gestures.

inspire players to make frequent stops and take their time. The rhythms at 7AM and 12PM can both be described as leisurely and sparse when compared to the frenetic and dense rhythm of *Vanquish*'s techno soundtrack, which mirrors the hectic action of gameplay that we explored in Chapter 2 (Figure 2.6). In general, the closer the alignment between rhythm and character steps, the greater the sense of synergy between music and gameplay.

The tonal quality of music in *Animal Crossing: New Leaf* and *Vanquish* complement their respective rhythm structures, which together create musical themes that describe the emotional state of the playable character and the player's physical gestures. However, rhythm (as well as tone and melody) may also describe the presence of a secondary character or location. In such cases, players are ambiently prompted to adjust their tempo to the musical signature of an impending obstacle or situation, as in the example of Bowser's castle theme in *Super Mario Bros.*, mentioned earlier. As we'll now see, the grounded aesthetics of rhythm and tempo have different effects on movement to that of melody.

Replay

Review gameplay footage of your favorite games—sequentially paying attention to tone, rhythm and tempo, and melody to aid you in your appreciation of each aesthetic concept in relation to gameplay. To get started, you may also wish to play through an entire 24-hour cycle in *Animal Crossing: A New Leaf* by Nintendo—or lookup "Animal Crossing: New Leaf Walkthrough" on YouTube—to appreciate how the music's changing rhythm and tempo affects the player's pace and activity. When analyzing video game music, it is often helpful to periodically close your eyes to help focus your sense of hearing.

Melody and Lines of Movement

While rhythm and tempo have the greatest influence on pacing, melody has the greatest effect on the buoyancy of the body—alluding to movement in the vertical axis (like the leaps of a ballerina across a stage), physical flight, or flights of the mind. In video game terms, this is reflected in the concepts that we explored in Chapter 2 where we compared the jump arcs and movement of playable characters in *Journey*, *INSIDE*, and *Vanquish*.

Melodic Contours

To establish a relationship between melody and gameplay we must examine the *melodic contour* that notes and pitches describe across a musical score. Melodic contours fall into three primary categories that echo our shape spectrum: curved (sinusoidal), square, and triangular. As you can see from Figure 7.6, melodic contours have a direct correlation with character lines of movement. Note that the illustrations in Figure 7.6 are to be used as a comparative analysis tool only, because melodies rarely align to each category with the same level of perfection.

Curved melodic contours support movement with a curved theme, such as the jump arcs of the traveler in *Journey* (Figure 2.3). Narrative-driven games with strictly linear character movement are less common. However, a title like *Monument Valley* (2014), by ustwo, demonstrates that linear movement is best supported by music featuring prolonged chords. Players would experience a sense of dissonance if *Monument Valley*'s soundtrack were based on curved or triangular melodic contours (Figure 7.7). Triangular melodic contours support aggressive lines of movement, like the example of *Vanquish* (Figure 2.6), which is at the extreme right end of the shape spectrum.

Even an untrained eye can see how the melodic contour in the fragment from the Overworld theme in *Super Mario Bros.* travels in a sinusoidal wave across

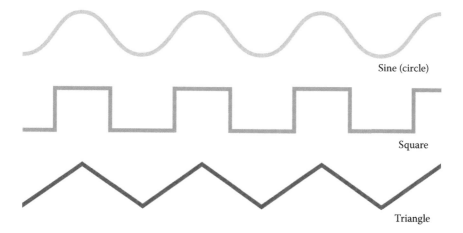

Sine (circle)

Square

Triangle

Figure 7.6 Sine (circle), square, and triangle melodic contours in music are directly correlated to our shape spectrum and character lines of movement.

Figure 7.7 Music based on circular or triangular melodic contours would be completely inappropriate for the character's predominantly linear lines of movement in *Monument Valley* (2014), by ustwo.

the page to reinforce the circular shape concept of Mario's character design and lines of movement (Figure 7.8). The outcome is a sense of harmony between Mario's Overworld theme and the playable character's jump abilities. The higher the amplitude (larger *intervallic* difference) of a melodic contour, the more suggestive it is of buoyant character movement or inspirational themes. If a bass beat describing rhythm is altogether absent, then the music becomes ethereal and flighty. Melodies with a shallow contour or those that place more emphasis on rhythm will naturally sound more grounded—like the rhythm-heavy soundtrack of *Vanquish*, which reflects the game's grounded gameplay.

Triangular Melodic Contours and Atonal Melodies

Mario's circular motif comes to an aesthetic head-to-head when players reach Bowser's castle and the archenemy's musical theme begins playing. The musical excerpt in Figure 7.9 illustrates the corresponding triangular melodic contour that describes an up and down sequence of notes that echo the famous theme from *Jaws* (1975), directed by Steven Spielberg. The full transcript also reveals a

Figure 7.8 The Overworld theme from *Super Mario Bros.* (1985), by Nintendo, exemplifies a curved melodic contour because of the flowing sequence of sounds that echo Mario's movement through levels (transcribed by BLUESCD).

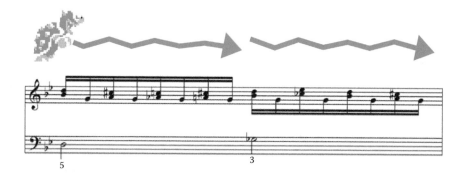

Figure 7.9 Bowser's Castle theme from *Super Mario Bros.* (1985), by Nintendo (transcribed by Joseph Karam), illustrates a triangular melodic contour and an atonal melody that creates player unease during encounters with Mario's arch-enemy, Bowser.

stampeding, *atonal* melodic theme, which is a term used to describe music that lacks a conventional sense of harmony—the melodic equivalent of a scrambling musical beat that has no discernible structure (known as *free time*). Triangular melodic contours and atonal melodies are used for boss battles in many Nintendo franchises—like *The Legend of Zelda* series—because the disjointed and jagged sequences of notes heighten the player's sense of agitation and reflect the psychological turmoil of the enemy encounter.

Musical Open Canvas

In Chapter 4 (Figure 4.5), we explored the concept of an "open canvas" to describe instances where the player is free to set his or her own path through an environment. In the context of audio, a similar concept occurs when the music stops:

players are either encouraged to pause their wanderings and contemplate, or are given free rein to enact their own unchoreographed actions within the confines of the playable character's animations and abilities. A world-class example of gameplay complemented by musical choreography and timely instances of quietness is explored in Chapter 13, Case Study: *Journey* section, which expertly harnesses the traits that distinguish rhythm and tempo from melody to create a dramatic musical progression that has the sophistication of a classical ballet performance.

Overt Drama versus Subtext

The reason that music firmly corresponds to the actions of playable characters is partly explained by interactivity and the manner in which gameplay is framed. The restrictions on camera settings that we discussed in Chapter 6, Framing, are a practical necessity for game design, which means that emotionally engaging close-ups of a character's facial expressions are difficult to implement during gameplay—when players are in control and have their attention fixed on events in the surrounding environment. As a result, gameplay music tends to focus on *overt drama*—drama that concerns the external manifestation of a character's inner feelings in the form of movement and physical activity. Take the example (Figure 7.10) from *Mass Effect 3* (2012), by BioWare, which features combat gameplay accompanied by an inspiring orchestral melody and forceful rhythm fitted to the pace of combat so that it closely matches the playable character's stride at running speed. When players sprint they experience the synergy between music

Figure 7.10 Video games and video game music tend to emphasize action over psychological drama partially because the playable character typically faces away from the camera in the direction of action—as in the combat sections of *Mass Effect 3* (2012), by BioWare, when the protagonist's facial expressions and inner thoughts are concealed.

and gameplay as an unintelligible sense of harmony, which abates whenever they slow to a walk. If the rhythm continued after the action had ceased—when all enemies have been dispatched—players would experience a sense of dissonance that is equivalent to dancers standing on an empty dance floor, motionless and without purpose, while dynamic music urges them to boogie on.

On the other hand, music in films and video game cutscenes has the ability to describe a wider range of drama because directors can freely cut between close-ups, mid-shots, and long-shots to frame the action from different perspectives. For instance, if the courageous facial expression of a stationary figure is captured with a dramatic close-up while an upbeat orchestral track begins playing, the audience will infer that the music reflects the character's state of mind—as in the epilogue cutscene from *Mass Effect 3* (Figure 7.11), which is viewed passively and does not rely on overt drama. The purpose for music in this context is to communicate *subtext*—psychological drama that concerns the thoughts and inner feelings of characters. The medium of video games has yet to evolve more sophisticated methods to reflect subtext during gameplay. As techniques for framing and editing gameplay continue to evolve, so too will opportunities to express internal drama.

Perhaps gaming's closest equivalent to internal drama communicated through sound is when rhythm reflects the player's heartbeat—not their footsteps. Assuming the context for gameplay has been sufficiently established, a high frequency of beats will suggest a faster heart rate and dramatic tension, while the action remains slow and ponderous. A well-known example is the motion tracker from the *Alien* franchise, and games like *Alien: Isolation* (2014), by Creative Assembly (Figure 7.12). The beeps emitted by the motion tracker clearly reference the sounds of hospital cardiac monitors, which assess a patient's condition relative to their cardiac rhythm. As the alien enemy moves closer, the motion tracker sounds the alarm by beeping with greater frequency, while gameplay encourages players to remain quiet and avoid excessive movement by keeping their footsteps muted to limit detection.

Figure 7.11 An example of music that expresses dramatic subtext is experienced during an epilogue cutscene in *Mass Effect 3* (2012), by BioWare, when Commander Shepard and Liara are seen reflecting on their somber victory to the accompaniment of a dramatic beat and inspiring orchestral track that denotes movement and heroism—despite their steadfast postures.

Figure 7.12 The motion tracker in *Alien: Isolation* (2014), by Creative Assembly, emits a pulse that increases in frequency when the alien gets closer, reflecting the player's heart rate, not the frequency of steps.

Silence

Complete silence, or the absence of music, is a very important aspect of a game's audio experience. Because music cues players to current or upcoming events, the absence of music means that they must defer to visual cues and their own sensibility. Gameplay situations without music feel more realistic since it is how we generally experience reality—increasing our reliance on visual stimuli from our surroundings and ambient sounds to shape how we feel.

Silence is a common feature in *The Last of Us* (2013), by Naughty Dog, which uses the absence of music to heighten the sense of loneliness for considerable durations of gameplay. As video game and audio designer, David Canela, puts it: "The fact that the audience can't rely on the music to warn it about what's going to happen next increases their sense of vulnerability." Consequently, the moments when music is introduced into gameplay take on greater significance and emotional impact. A game's audio should therefore include moments of silence to reflect the same level of depth as the visual and interactive concepts that we've explored in previous chapters. Silence is as important to audio as negative space is to visual art.

Diegetic and Non-Diegetic Sound Effects

A powerful accompaniment to music and immersion is the acoustic space of sound effects. Video game sound effects include diegetic sounds (sounds that occur from sources *inside* the game world) and non-diegetic sounds (sounds that occur *outside* the game world). Examples of diegetic sounds include voices of in-game characters, music emanating from a radio located in the environment, and the sounds of objects audibly interacting with each other in a believable way. Non-diegetic sound effects include a narrator's commentary or sound added for dramatic effect.

The concept of tone, which we explored earlier, is straightforward to apply to both categories of sound effects. Sounds aligned to circular aesthetics prompt players to perform soft gestures and elicit a positive sense of well-being; square sounds call for stillness and calm; and triangular sounds aesthetically dial the player's actions and emotions toward a snappier and more aggressive state. A familiar example can be found in popular TV game shows where the upward trill of a contestant's correct answer is contrasted by the downward blast of a wrong answer.

The function of diegetic sound effects goes beyond giving players a sense of acoustic realism and presence within the game world. In fact, the concept of dancing is no less applicable to sound effects than it is to music because sound effects act as an organic substitute for tones, rhythm, and tempo. Like an abstract jazz piece without a distinct melody, the playable character's footsteps define a fitful beat, while sounds emanating from the environment provide the musical tones. *The Last of Us* sets a great example for the application of sound effects to compliment the visual and interactive elements of gameplay (Figure 7.13). During low-tension moments in the narrative, the mood is conveyed through sound effects that have a positive, circular tone, like birds chirping, a slight breeze, and the rustle of vegetation.

Figure 7.13 Tender moments between the two protagonists in *The Last of Us* (2013), by Naughty Dog—like the zoo scene shown here—are supported by sound effects based on positive and harmonious circular tones that emanate from objects in the environment.

(a)   (b)

Figure 7.14 A moment of acoustic stillness in *The Last of Us* (2013), by Naughty Dog, expertly counters players' expectations for a surprise conflict (a), which does not materialize until later in the level when it is ushered in by a medley of sound effects with triangular tones (b).

During neutral, explorative sections of gameplay in *The Last of Us*, little more than the playable character's footsteps can be heard reverberating off the walls while the environment reflects a square-like acoustic stillness. These moments of relative stillness can take on a positive or negative meaning because the brief lull in narrative tension suggests that events are ready to swing toward a positive or negative state—like the illusory sense of calm during a Mexican standoff. A sound effect as subtle as the squawk of a crow can suddenly shift the atmosphere toward a triangular theme, as the action becomes increasingly confrontational to the accompaniment of a wailing siren and the clicks and shrieks of infected enemies (Figure 7.14).

Not all the sources of diegetic sounds need to be visually accounted for in-game, since certain objects need only be alluded to—such as a bird song, for instance. However, it goes without saying that diegetic sound effects should be developed in concert with interactive and visual assets if they're to support the aesthetic requirement of the narrative to the same extent as other disciplines on the game development team.

Video Game Accompanists

While we can aptly relate player activity to that of a dancer responding to music, the role of game audio designers has a clear resemblance to silent film accompanists (Figure 7.15). Musicians in this field once played to the likes of Buster Keaton (1895–1966) and Charlie Chaplin (1889–1977) films; however, the discipline remains very much alive and continues to evolve. Contemporary accompanists act as the musical bridge between the audience and the action on-screen—making sure the audience remains immersed in the unfolding drama without being distracted by the music. The guiding principle for accompanist and historian, Ben Model, is to play music that is "pretty enough to listen to, but not interesting enough to pay attention to." Accompanists either improvise or use

Figure 7.15 Accompanists from the silent film era used accentuation and impromptu notes during live performances to amplify the action being projected on-screen—mirroring the role that audio designers and players have in authoring and activating video game music and sound effects.

existing pieces of music that are chosen for their function, not stylistic value, so that the music can be easily coaxed to reflect the dramatic events of the film. They often sit facing the cinema screen with one ear on the audience and interpret the film's action as if it were music notation—*matching* an escalation in drama with a build up in the music; adding a musical inflection; or a crashing chord at the exact moment of an actor's comic gesture. If the accompanist feels that the audience is losing interest, she can re-engage filmgoers by simplifying the music or dropping the volume—mirroring the rhetorical technique of speaking quietly to draw in listeners.

Audio designers working in video games face the same challenges of portraying the playable character's movements through music and amplifying actions with sound effects. A composer must work with animators, game designers, and scriptwriters to ascertain in advance the playable character's varied emotional states, stride tempo, and abilities to determine the music that will accompany players as they traverse the game's narrative—much like the accompanist deciding which song will best fit the action of a silent film. The accompanist's spontaneous accentuations and impromptu notes that underline special events are equivalent to in-game sound effects that are designed by audio teams but activated spontaneously by players during gameplay as their playable character "dances" across the screen.

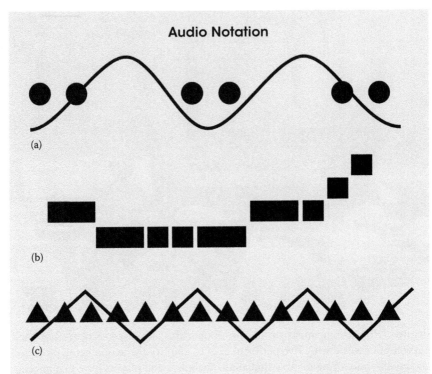

Audio Notation

(a)

(b)

(c)

Tone and rhythm can be visualized in combination using the same notation that we will explore for player gestures in the following chapter—underlining the synergy between the two elements of dynamic composition. Melodic contours can be superimposed over the notation for tone and rhythm using a simple line that can be drawn as a sine, square, or triangular contour. For instance, slow and gentle beats (*Animal Crossing: New Leaf*) can be illustrated using circles that are spaced at regular intervals to indicate positive tones and a gentle rhythm that is complimented by a flowing melody (a). When only one instrument or sound is present, then tone, rhythm, and melody can be combined into one pictorial sequence of shapes (b). An aggressive and persistent rhythm (*Vanquish*) can be described using triangles, and overlaid with an angular line indicating a triangular melodic contour (c).

Summary

The above concepts of tone, rhythm and tempo, melody and musical harmony allow us to create characters inspired by music. Working the other way, the same concepts can be used to paint musical portraits of existing characters based on their signature movements and on-screen activity. As David Kanaga, the composer behind *Proteus* (2013), and *Panoramical* (2015), puts it:

There's all these really detailed time structures happening in games. So when I'm doing music I try to think, ok, the game already has time structures in place, and the goal of the music oughta be to just hug that as tightly as possible.

Dancing is music made visible and the reason why video game environments—much like a dance floor—can be conceptualized as a stage for player-expression. Virtual reality and interactive experiences that engage the player's entire body will bring together the concept of character movement and dancing even closer together. Tone plays a key role in shaping the player's gestures because the aesthetics of sound correlate with our primary shapes, which we primarily use for comparative analysis. Rhythm and tempo sets the structure for action and gives it a grounded feeling—echoing the footsteps of a character or the player's heartbeat. Music driven by melody and musical harmony communicates an ethereal and flighty feeling. For added depth, audio can always be juxtaposed or deliberately misleading for artistic effect.

The fluidity with which music can change from moment-to-moment is a great asset for game design, which usually requires that a single set of animations is used consistently to avoid interactions between the playable character and the environment from breaking (see discussion on Figure 2.11). Music suggests nuances of movement, even if no variations are present in-game (Figure 7.4). Music can also be used to foreshadow events or for orientation purposes—such as the use of automated triggers in the environment that activate sounds when the player approaches.

We are now just one chapter away from applying our understanding of primary shapes and dynamic composition to the orchestration of emotionally rich interactive stories. The final element of dynamic composition discusses how the cumulative effects of character shapes and poses, lines of movement, environment shapes, pathways, framing, and audio influence the player's gestures, which are the most distinct feature of video games as an art form.

8 Player Gestures

In Chapter 1, we discovered that the design of a character serves as an important visual cue to their personality and emotional state. This concept derives from the behaviors of real people who likewise externalize their inner feelings through outward forms of expression. What makes video gaming's element of interactivity so significant is that it allows designers to work in reverse: influencing the gestures of players that, in turn, affect their emotional state. It's for this very reason that we assigned so much importance to synchronized characters in Chapter 2, because they directly influence the player's physical gestures and sense of well-being. In this sense, the player is akin to a music conductor who activates and guides the orchestra, while simultaneously responding to the music with gestures that vary in accordance to the changing aesthetics of the musical composition. A playable character's fluidity of movement should therefore be a priority to ensure that the game's storytelling capabilities are equally fluid. Poorly implemented controls or controls that are not aligned with the narrative will result in players feeling a sense of dissonance that limits their level of immersion.

Calibration and Synchronization

The most direct way to experience gesture-narrative dissonance is by playing a game in the first-person exploration genre with a focus on peaceful, non-confrontational gameplay. Such games use conventional mouse input for panning the in-game camera, just like any other first-person shooter game. Therefore, even if the game has been designed to evoke feelings of calm, you will nonetheless find that you can aggressively pan the first-person view by shaking the mouse

Replay

Play through your favorite first-person games—anything from the *Halo* series to *The Beginner's Guide*—paying particular attention to the predefined pace of the disembodied playable character. If the character has a slow pace, try traversing the environment while panning the camera with quick and sharp gestures. Conversely, if the game has a fast combative theme, make delicate adjustments to the camera while moving around.

left and right—in opposition to the aesthetic intentions of the game's designers. This simple exercise serves to highlight the fine balance between player autonomy and predefined aesthetics. If players are to perform gestures that align with the implied behavior and emotional state of their virtual character, it's essential that unwanted forms of expression are restricted, and character movements and camera responsiveness are calibrated to support the game's narrative. Otherwise, players may experience a sense of dissonance when their virtual head seemingly belongs to a *Quake* deathmatch contestant while their stride references the pace of a villager from the *Animal Crossing* series. Note that this awareness of gesture-narrative dissonance applies to all games—irrespective of their genre—where the designers wish to create a specific mood.

Player-Character Synchronization

Dissonance can also occur if the player is not given a convincing impulse to act, even though the narrative may involve a time-critical event. In such cases, it is advisable to introduce gameplay mechanisms that motivate action, such as a collapsing platform (Figure 8.1a), a moving vehicle, a closing gate (Figure 8.1b), or advancing enemies. Without such devices, there is a danger that players remain impassive while the game world collapses around them. Such devices can also be helpful in setting a direction for action by pointing players toward the next important story event.

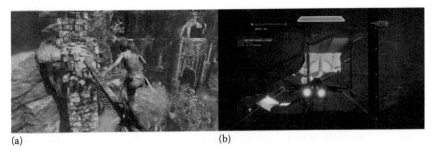

(a)   (b)

Figure 8.1 Environment events can be used to activate players and set a direction for gameplay, such as a collapsing platform in *Rise of the Tomb Raider* (2015) by Crystal Dynamics (a), or a closing gate in *Halo 4* (2012) by 343 Industries (b).

Figure 8.2 A strong sense of player-character empathy is generated in *Shadow of the Colossus* (2005), by Team Ico, because the player's gesture of holding down the R1 button on the PlayStation controller echoes the playable character's action of holding onto the colossus.

In a typical console game, a character's movements are triggered by the player's thumb swipes on an analog stick. These seemingly subtle movements of the thumb readily ripple out to other parts of the body, so that the player's arms, shoulders, and upper body begin to reverberate the actions of their on-screen character. *Shadow of the Colossus* (2005), by Fumito Ueda, features many such examples of player-character harmony. Players must hold down the R1 shoulder button of the PlayStation controller whenever they wish to grasp the hide of a moving colossus. The act of gripping the controller while keeping the R1 button pressed physically echoes the action of the in-game character, Wander, as he holds on (Figure 8.2). And, like Wander, this sustained action causes players to become physically tired as they scramble to mount the colossi with additional taps of the △ button to propel them upward.

The final sword stabs needed to bring down the colossi in *Shadow of the Colossus* have also been artistically timed to give a sense of drama. The player cannot freely mash the □ button to thrust the sword. Instead, Fumito Ueda designed the interaction so that players must first initiate a dramatic raising of the sword through a prolonged press of the □ button before they are able to plunge it into the colossi's hide with a final executing tap (Figure 8.3).

Player Gestures and Game Controllers

An influential book on the topic of player gestures is *Game Feel: A Game Designer's Guide to Virtual Sensation* (CRC Press, 2009), by Steve Swink. The author highlights the level of attention to detail required to craft a sophisticated interactive experience in the following analysis of the Nintendo 64 controller (Figure 8.4):

The shoulder buttons and Z-button on the bottom of the controller are slightly poppier than those on the front of the controller, reaching their depressed state

Figure 8.3 The action of taking down the colossi in *Shadow of the Colossus*, by Team Ico, is dramatically heightened because players must first hold down the ☐ button to raise the protagonist's sword before delivering the final stab of the sword.

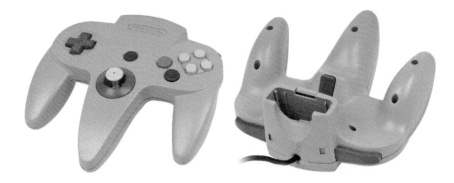

Figure 8.4 Steve Swink's detailed analysis of the Nintendo 64 controller illustrates the attention to detail required when designing around player gestures, which should be treated with as much subtlety as that of a musician playing a delicate instrument.

more quickly. The analog thumbstick, the first of its kind to be included in a mass produced highly successful controller, feels a little crusty by today's standards, almost like there's fine sandpaper in the base of it. It's also longer and includes a much more powerful spring than modern controllers' thumbsticks. Compared to the thumbsticks in my Xbox 360 and PlayStation 2 controllers, the spring seems to take roughly twice as much force to displace. Movements feel much more emphatic and the pushback of the stick against my thumb is much more noticeable. As a result, players receive more proprioceptive feedback and can more accurately gauge movements between full on and full off.

Concurrently, such a sensitive design approach could make the difference between mapping certain actions to the snappy L1 and R1 triggers on the PlayStation DualShock®4 controller (Figure 8.5), or the gentler L2 and R2 shoulder buttons that have significantly more leeway when pressed. It's better to think of video game controllers as sophisticated instruments to be tuned to a story's requirements, rather than simple input devices.

In this respect, British video game developer, Media Molecule, deserves an honorable mention because it has made it somewhat of a manifesto to explore the functionality of input devices in novel ways. Whether using the built-in camera and rear-facing touchpad of the PlayStation Vita in *Tearaway* (2013) (Figure 8.6) or the PlayStation Move to control in-game characters like real-life puppets, Media Molecule's games often enhance the tactile experience of interaction with in-game objects—dissolving the disconnect between the player's physical gestures and the virtual world.

Swink's analysis of the Nintendo 64 controller extends to the platform's flagship game, *Super Mario 64* (1996). Swink highlights the particularly elegant example of player-character harmony that the game achieves because the turning radius of the analog stick on the Nintendo 64 controller closely matches the turning radius of Mario in-game (Figure 8.7). This example of *natural mapping* makes *Super Mario 64*'s control scheme feel exceptionally intuitive because of

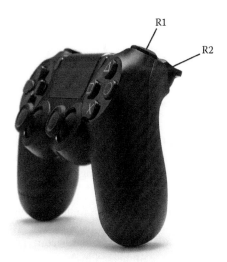

Figure 8.5 Every game controller has a unique set of design considerations, such as the varied responsiveness between the L1/R1 and L2/R2 shoulder buttons on the PlayStation DualShock 4 controller—determining which buttons are assigned to certain actions.

Figure 8.6 *Tearaway* (2013), by Media Molecule, allows players to tap the rear-facing touchpad of the PlayStation Vita to interact with in-game enemies—with the player's fingers seemingly piercing the virtual environment.

Figure 8.7 *Super Mario 64* (1996), by Nintendo, is celebrated for its intuitive control scheme because Mario's turning radius in-game is closely mapped to the turning radius of the N64 controller's analog stick.

the 1-to-1 translation of real-world gestures to in-game movement. When controls are perfectly mapped, players experience disassociation from their own body and project their sense of self onto the on-screen avatar. The controller fades from their conscious as they become immersed in the virtual world.

Motion Controllers

Motion controllers—such as Microsoft's Kinect, the Touch controller for Oculus Rift, and Nintendo's Wii Remote—offer a greater range of possibilities for synchronization between player and character. Compare the differing control sensations for two games that use Nintendo's Wii Remote: *Mario Kart 8* (2014), and *Tron: Evolution* (2010) (Figure 8.8a,b). The forgiving vehicle handling and rounded tracks of *Mario Kart 8* have the player tilting the controller using gentler physical gestures that reference the circle shape concept. The abrupt handling of *Tron*'s Light Cycles reference the abrupt turns seen in the original Disney movie, which result in players using correspondingly sharper physical gestures to control the vehicles.

French developer, Quantic Dream, is known for paying particular attention to the performative aspect of the player's role in video games. The control scheme in games like *Heavy Rain* (2010), and *Beyond Two Souls* (2013) have players responding to on-screen prompts that direct them to enact the motions of their character as closely as possible. A heightened example of player-character harmony is experienced if the games are played with the PlayStation Move controller, which directs players to perform natural gestures like thrusting the controller forward to have the in-game protagonist knock on a door (Figure 8.9).

(a)   (b)

Figure 8.8 *Mario Kart 8* (2014), by Nintendo (a) features vehicles that have forgiving vehicle handling compared to the highly responsive light cycles in *Tron: Evolution* (2010), by Propaganda Games (b).

Figure 8.9 *Heavy Rain* (2010), by Quantic Dream, uses the PlayStation Move controller to great effect by having players mirror the actions of the on-screen character to heighten player-character empathy.

Figure 8.10 The Void is the world's first virtual reality theme park—providing visitors with an unprecedented level of immersion and tactile, physical experiences by combining virtual reality environments that are mapped to real-world props.

Virtual Reality

The burgeoning field of virtual reality promises to go a step further in eliciting full-body gestures and tactile interactions that make the "holodeck" from *Star Trek* a reality. For instance, the pioneering work of The Void—a Utah-based outfit behind the first virtual reality theme park—enables players to explore virtual worlds built over physical environments (Figure 8.10). The player's body is tracked in real time in relation to real-world props like walls, wind, and sprays of water—all of which have digital counterparts that are experienced through a virtual reality headset. The concept of natural mapping becomes even more critical with virtual reality because camera movements, for instance, that don't align with the player's actions or expectations are a surefire way to induce motion sickness.

Keeping Controls Simple

Keep in mind that more interactivity does not necessarily make a better game. Not all the buttons of a controller must be assigned an action, as simple inputs are easier for players to manipulate and can therefore increase immersion. thatgamecompany's cofounder and creative director, Jenova Chen, believes that controllers can get in the way of gameplay. In an interview with Ryan Clements (IGN 2011), Chen explained that his perfect controller would be "like the original NES controller: a d-pad and two buttons. Simple. With modern controllers, leaving a button or stick untouched seems like a missed opportunity for more precise control, but perhaps these 'precise controls' just complicate things."

Player Gesture Notation

Swipes

Button taps

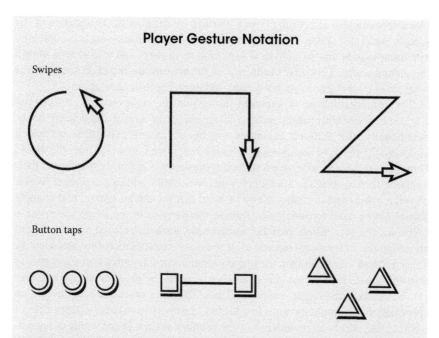

The notation for player gestures includes swipes to indicate movements of the player's arms or analog stick, and button taps. Swipes are sketched with a standard mouse cursor and a trailing line that references the primary shapes. Button icons are used for tap gestures by adding a drop-shadow to each primary shape. Circular buttons can indicate soft or playful taps, square buttons for prolonged holds, and triangles for aggressive button mashing.

Summary

Player gestures are arguably the most important element of dynamic composition because they epitomize video gaming's eminent artistic feature: interaction. Orchestrating the player's gestures to reflect on-screen activity is so essential to interactive storytelling that it is advisable that the design process starts with an outline of the desired physical gestures that players should experience before going about designing game mechanics that elicit those gestures. Take a moment to review the previous chapters of this book to reaffirm each element of dynamic composition in the context of player gestures. It is also important to analyze the various control inputs for each game controller to gain a stronger understanding for the particularities of each platform. Understanding such subtleties is essential if players are to attain a heightened sense of empathy with their playable character. This is achieved by modulating a character's lines of movement to reflect the circular, linear, or angular motions—as we saw in games like *Journey, INSIDE,* and *Vanquish* in Chapter 2. Pathways in the environment and secondary nonplayable characters can also affect the player's gestures by defining the boundaries of the game's explorable space. The complement of haptic feedback—such as controller vibrations—adds an extra physical sensation to impacts and interactions within the virtual world. This direct influence of the artwork on the player-audience is what makes video games such a unique and engaging artistic medium.

The concepts that we've explored throughout the eight chapters of dynamic composition certainly won't make you an expert in any of the related fields. Additionally, the featured examples are by no means exhaustive, so you'll undoubtedly think of many worthy cases that didn't make it into the book. However, you should now have a sufficient sensitivity to primary shapes and their aesthetic themes to make studies of your own—both within the virtual worlds of video games and in reality. Keep in mind that the circle, square, and triangle should not be used formulaically. Rather, the purpose of the shape spectrum is to inspire and give insight into the fundamental aesthetics of design that apply to all design disciplines—giving you tools to assess shape relationships and identify areas that lack clarity. In fact, turning conventions upside-down is encouraged, as this will create unexpected situations that surprise the player-audience and create characters with greater emotional depth. The main objective is to develop an appreciation for simplicity and a heightened sensitivity to shapes—irrespective of whether they neatly align with one of the primary shapes. In the words of legendary animation production designer, Hans Bacher:

> Overloading the frame with too much detail means the eye doesn't know where to look. [...] Same goes with ideas. Don't try to put too many ideas into a single image. This makes the composition muddy and confusing. Not a good strategy for film where the audience only has a few seconds to interpret each shot. Say one thing with one shot and use a different shot to say something else.

In games, the player-audience has even more information to interpret than in film and animation considering the added task of interactivity in response to on-screen events. Simplicity is therefore the key to ensuring that communication of aesthetic concepts is quick and accessible. The three primary shapes are therefore perfectly suited to convey ideas in a simple manner.

The conclusion of our investigation into primary shapes and dynamic composition means that we are ready to tackle the advanced challenge of examining how video games can be orchestrated into a symphony of interactivity, game art, and audio with the help of the dramatic curve and transitions. As stated by the influential Russian abstract painter, Wassily Kandinsky (1866–1944): "the content of a work of art finds its expression in the composition ... in the sum of the tensions inwardly organized for the work." In other words, it is one thing to understand the aesthetic value of individual shapes, but an artwork's true meaning—its message—is the outcome of the relationships between the elements within the frame or gameplay space. Before we explore dynamic composition in the context of storytelling, we will make a brief segue to explore transitions in films so that we have a clear understanding for the function of dramatic curves and transitions before considering their application in video games.

II

The Dramatic Curve
and Transitions

In the following pages we will explore the dramatic curve, which is the most widely used narrative structure across all storytelling media. The dramatic curve has several inherent functions that address the audience's limited ability to emotionally and mentally process large amounts of plot information. Transitions—the aesthetic changes across two adjoining scenes—will help us to understand how stories can be delivered in a way that heightens the emotional experience of the dramatic curve.

This section explores the dramatic curve's application in film and presents an especially bold example of its base functions so that we can better understand its value for storytelling. Our examination of the dramatic curve and transitions will

then be adapted to video games in subsequent chapters—providing us with a framework for analyzing the emotional effectiveness and clarity of interactive stories.

Narrative Tension

Most stories have the same basic structure, which follows the journey of a protagonist who struggles against opposition to reach a goal that may, or may not, be
resolved. The journey of Frodo, played by Elijah Wood, in *The Lord of the Rings* film
trilogy (2001–2003)—based on the novel by J. R. R. Tolkien—is a familiar example
of this narrative structure (Figure SII.1). Frodo and his companions must overcome
a series of physical and psychological obstacles that force them from the safety of
their *round* Hobbit holes in the Shire, towards the story's climax within the *jagged*

(a)

(b)

(c)

Figure SII.1 *The Lord of the Rings* trilogy (2001–2003), New Line Cinema,
directed by Peter Jackson. From (a–c): Frodo must depart the safety of the Shire
and overcome hazardous obstacles that gradually raise tension to a dramatic climax at the trilogy's end.

depths of Mount Doom. To set the perfect stage for this important point of narrative resolution, director Peter Jackson carefully orchestrated a build up of tension over the course of the three films to create a dramatic climax at the moment that Frodo contemplates the final destruction of the Ring. Peter Jackson increased tension using principles of cinematography that overlap with the concepts that we explored in previous chapters concerning the shape spectrum and dynamic composition.

To understand the purpose of raising tension toward a film's climax, let's consider the alternative (Figure SII.2). Here we have a story in which the narrative tension remains constant throughout. Where do you, as the storyteller, place the most important narrative events? It's relatively insignificant where you place key elements of your story along such a monotonous tension line as they will likely be overlooked if the audience cannot anticipate them. Without pacing characterized by periods of high and low activity, the audience begins to experience *vigilance fatigue*.

You can get a sense for vigilance fatigue if you imagine reading a novel in which punctuation and capital letters have been entirely removed. Reading such a piece of text would be confusing and overwhelmingly tiresome because you'd spend more effort trying to locate the end of each sentence than you would on the story. You can therefore think of scene transitions as a form of punctuation that makes it easier to discern a film's (or video game's) key plot points.

Effective storytelling relies on the storyteller's ability to deliver a narrative in a way that supports the audience's ability to orient its way through a narrative, which is achieved with the dramatic curve illustrated in Figure SII.3. The dramatic curve is applicable to the overarching narrative as well as a scene-by-scene basis. Along this curve we find two important events: a *call-to-action* (Frodo is impelled to travel to Mount Doom and destroy the Ring) and a *turning point* (against all odds, Frodo succeeds in destroying the Ring). The call-to-action establishes the context for the drama and mounting tension that follows, which has the purpose of alerting the audience to an impending turn of events. Without a rise in tension

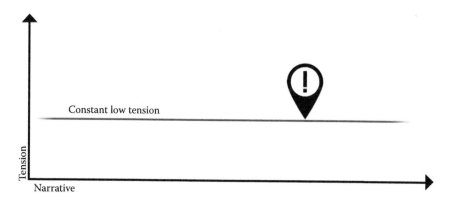

Figure SII.2 A narrative with a flat tension line means that the audience is not primed to anticipate important story events because everything appears to be of equal importance.

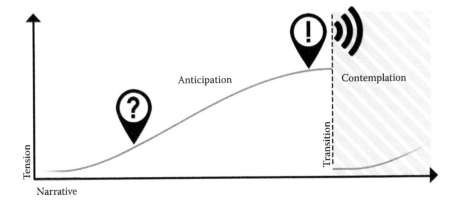

Figure SII.3 The dramatic curve primes the audience to anticipate an important turning point and creates an emotionally resonant moment of contemplation after the transition.

the audience cannot mentally and emotionally prepare for the important turning point. A dramatic event is significantly more effective if the audience can evoke the appropriate emotions beforehand—so that the actual event serves more to validate or subvert the audience's imaginings, rather than dictating their experience.

You may recognize the dramatic curve if you're familiar with the classic three-act structure, or the work of Joseph Campbell and the monomyth. The interactive and nonsequential nature of video games means that game developers cannot readily adopt these classical narrative structures, as they were developed for linear, noninteractive media. We will therefore focus on the dramatic curve's functions that support player agency and nonlinear storytelling.

Emotionally Resonant Transitions in Film

The transition represents the passage between two scenes. The sequence of stills in Figure SII.4 from *The Lord of the Rings: The Two Towers* (2002) is a text-book example of an emotionally rich transition. The scene before the transition is set on a cold, blue dawn, and begins with an argument between orcs and goblins (Figure SII.4a,b, who have captured the hobbits, Merry and Pippin (played by Dominic Monaghan and Billy Boyd, respectively). The two hobbits use the ensuing disorder (Figure SII.4c) to make their escape (Figure SII.4d), which denotes the call-to-action for the scene. Activity quickly escalates to an all-out battle when the silhouetted Riders of Rohan arrive to slaughter the orcs and goblins (Figure SII.4e,f)—framed by a dynamic camera that sharply pans left, right, left as it traces flying arrows and swords slash across the screen. The turning point signals the final moment of the scene, when narrative tension is at its highest and Pippin is seemingly trampled by a horse (Figure SII.4g,h).

Just at this moment a sudden inversion of aesthetics occurs between the scenes on either side of the transition. Against a quiet landscape bathed in the warm light of sunrise we see the figure of Legolas (Figure SII.5), played by Orlando Bloom,

Figure SII.4 *The Lord of the Rings: The Two Towers* (2002), New Line Cinema, directed by Peter Jackson. The above scene is a textbook implementation of the dramatic curve that features a call-to-action and building tension toward a climactic turning point.

Figure SII.5 *The Lord of the Rings: The Two Towers* (2002), New Line Cinema, directed by Peter Jackson. The beginning of the scene after the transition is designed to aesthetically contrast preceding events in order to create an emotional echo and provide the audience with a quiet moment of contemplation.

come to a standstill to contemplatively whisper: "Red sun rises. Blood has been spilt this night." Director, Peter Jackson, carefully orchestrated this moment so that Legolas underlines the very thoughts that we—the audience—are compelled to ask through *deductive reasoning*: *whose* blood has been spilt this night? The orchestration of this transition summarizes an essential concern for the director's craft that involves planting intriguing questions and delaying disclosure until later in the film.

Anticipation of Important Events

For the audience to engage in a narrative it must be suitably primed to anticipate important story events—such as whether Merry and Pippin will make good on their plan to escape (Figure SII.4d). The cinematography and audio reach their highest dramatic tension at the end of the scene—just before the transition—ensuring that the audience is eager and ready for the turning point that promises to provide an answer, or spin the drama in a new direction. Entertainment is derived from the unexpected nature of this turning point. The scene that follows the transition (Figure SII.5) serves as a quiet space of low activity in which the audience can contemplate events before tension is ramped up again. What makes scene-to-scene transitions so important in this respect is that they add emotional emphasis and clarity to the story (Figure SII.6).

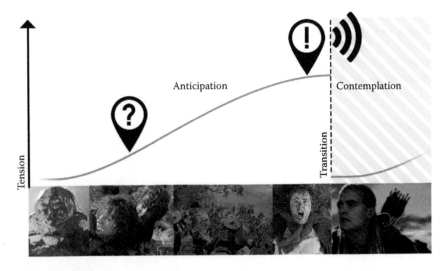

Figure SII.6 The dramatic curve for the featured transition from *The Lord of the Rings: The Two Towers* (2002) highlights the call-to-action, turning point, and aesthetic contrast between the adjoining scenes.

The Primary Functions of a Transition

A transition has the following primary functions, which are supported by the aesthetics that occur along the dramatic curve:

Call-to-action (before transition): an inciting event sets the context for ensuing drama

Mounting tension (before): tension is gradually ramped up to prime the audience to anticipate a key event in the story

Turning point (before): presents a revelation or significant turn of events

Contemplative space (after): for contemplating the turning point and the narrative as a whole

Contrasting aesthetics (before and after): used to heighten the *emotional echo*

Of more significance to the emotional experience of the story is the inversion of aesthetics across the transition. In *The Lord of the Rings* example above, the contemplative space of low-activity after the transition (Figure SII.5) amplifies the high-tension aesthetics that concluded the previous scene (Figure SII.4). The stronger the aesthetic contrast between adjoining scenes, the stronger the emotional echo experienced by the audience, who continues to feel the emotional reverberations in which we last saw Pippin beneath the hooves of the horse. In his essential book, *Between the Scenes: What Every Film Director, Writer, and Editor Should Know about Scene Transitions* (2014), film director Jeffrey Michael Bay describes the emotional echo as a wave of plot intensity and emotion, which breaks onto the empty space of contemplation that follows the transition. Transitions need not be as action-packed as the above example. Subtler narratives will naturally call for subtler transitions, as will intermediate story events that link the major turning points of the film.

Replay

The Lord of the Rings: The Two Towers (2002), New Line Cinema, directed by Peter Jackson.

You'll find the transition featured across Figures SII.4 and SII.5 *The Lord of the Rings: The Two Towers* at roughly 21 minutes into the film. Alternatively, you're welcome to visit www.solarskistudio.com/videos to examine the above transition. Pay particular attention to the inversion of aesthetics across the transition and how the contemplative space allows the emotions of Pippin's apparent death to be amplified.

Summary

The dramatic structure illustrated above is the most commonly used structure for storytelling because it has been refined over millennia to address humankind's inherent ability to process and emotionally experience information. For this reason you'll find it embedded across all popular media where it is used to engage the broadest demographic possible. To paraphrase a key message in *Understanding Comics: The Invisible Art* (HarperPerennial 1994), by Scott McCloud:

> It's between the two scenes [or panels of a comic book] that stories and emotions are awoken—and nourished by aesthetic contrast—in the viewer's mind.

This is not to say that every narrative must follow this structure. However, by understanding the significance of its functions you'll be better positioned to assess potential consequences whenever deviating from convention.

Now that we understand the mechanics of the dramatic curve and transitions—and the importance of anticipation, contemplation, and contrast—we can go about adapting the above concepts to video games with the help of all the techniques that we covered in dynamic composition. The following chapter will highlight special considerations for structuring the dramatic curve in video games, such as the mentally intensive demands of interactivity.

9 Transitions in Games

In films we say: show, don't tell.
In games we say: do, don't show.

Jeremy Bernstein
Game Designer

Images are far more effective at expressing a story than dialogue or text because as much as 80% of human interaction is transmitted through the sense of sight. Dialogue should only be used in support of the visual story—hence, the film industry's motto: "show, don't tell." What sets video games apart from other storytelling mediums is the active participation of the player-audience. Hence, Jeremy Bernstein's guiding principle of "do, don't show," which prioritizes player activity over visuals and dialogue. Video games certainly do a lot of "showing," as we explored in dynamic composition. However, the maxim nicely summarizes a fundamental design principle for the game development industry. Because the player-audience has the added task of interacting with the story—the task of actively *doing* things—the concepts of anticipation and contemplation that we explored in the previous section must be treated with even more sensitivity than for film.

Deductive Reasoning and Real-Time Gameplay

Another consideration when translating film storytelling techniques to games is the purpose of film editing as a means to infer meaningful events that occur beyond the frame. Editing encourages the audience to engage with the narrative through deductive reasoning, which involves actively piecing together absolute and incomplete pieces of information to make personal assumptions about the

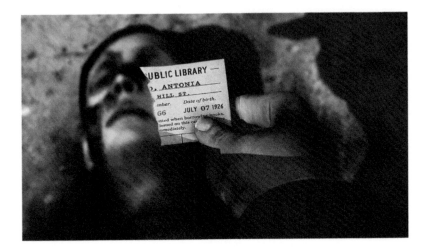

Figure 9.1 The detective gameplay of *L.A. Noire* (2011), by Rockstar Games, naturally promotes deductive reasoning because clues discovered during the course of play allude to sinister activity that occurred outside the frame.

plot. In contrast, when a player is engaged in gameplay they usually experience every moment of a narrative in *real time* (which accounts for the longer completion times of most games versus a typical film). Players engage in deductive reasoning nonetheless because of their subjective perspective of the narrative, which is perceived through the eyes of their playable character. Detective games like *L.A. Noire* (2011), by Rockstar Games, innately encourage the phenomenon because each newly acquired clue has the potential to reshape the player's understanding of events based on their assessment of evidence (Figure 9.1).

The player-audience will engage in deductive reasoning more frequently when story elements are alluded to without being explained outright—as in games like *LIMBO* (2010) (Figure 9.2), and *Bloodborne* (2015), which present narrative cues through secondary characters and environmental storytelling but stop short of disclosing specific meaning.

The Unreliable Gamemaster

Due to the constraints of storytelling in real time—which can lead to an overabundance of absolute narrative information—games must continue to evolve with techniques that reshape the player's perception of the plot on the fly. The benefits are clear: as we've seen with film editing, the artistic value of deductive reasoning can far exceed the sum of a game's parts when players are invited to contribute their own imaginings to the narrative. The most effective technique for eliciting such experiences is based on the concept of an *unreliable gamemaster*. An unreliable gamemaster is perceived as an untrustworthy or mischievous game designer that commits players to quests with dubious objectives—thus challenging gaming's propensity for defined rules and victory conditions. The role is similar to that of a film director that undermines the audience's expectations with

Figure 9.2 The presence of hostile secondary characters in *LIMBO* (2010), by Playdead, is never explained—leaving players to draw their own conclusions about their significance in the narrative.

a plot twist. The unreliable gamemaster's motives can likewise be compromised from the outset or delayed until the end of the game for greater dramatic effect.

Games like *Shadow of the Colossus* (2005) by Team Ico, *Braid* (2008) by Number None, Inc., and *The Last of Us* (2013) by Naughty Dog, commit players to quests that dupe them into expecting a certain outcome that is eventually countered by a surprise revelation. The unreliable narrator can also assume an active presence in-game when cast as a direct antagonist to players. For example, the unreliable gamemaster in *The Stanley Parable* (2011), by Galactic Cafe, is personified by a narrator who accounts every decision that players make, despite their best efforts to subvert the "proper path" of the narrative (Figure 9.3).

The critical success of games that feature variations on the unreliable gamemaster is a testament to the enjoyment that players derive from having their wits tested by an antagonist-game designer. We will explore the concept in more detail in a case study of *Gone Home* (2013) by The Fullbright Company in Chapter 13.

Editing-Out Inconsequential Events

It's worth noting that film editing's second function—to condense time by eliminating inconsequential scenes—has a video game counterpart that comes in the form of *power-ups* and teleportation mechanics. These functional relatives of film editing likewise extricate the need for players to concern themselves with mundane activities: teleportation mechanics allow players to travel long distances in a flash; and power-ups grant abilities to instantly heal playable characters, increase their strength, or acquire new skills and abilities. Alternatively, games can simply ignore conventional human needs—such as in *Ico* (2001), in which the playable character never eats, drinks, or tires because the game's designer, Fumito Ueda, wished to focus on the protagonist's quest to escape the confines of the castle (Figure 9.4).

Figure 9.3 The concept of a trustworthy game designer is cast aside in *The Stanley Parable* (2011), by Galactic Cafe, in which players are led like puppets through the game's narrative despite their best efforts to subvert proceedings.

Figure 9.4 Game designers can take artistic license and conveniently overlook time-sapping human needs like food and health to focus on the core narrative—as in *Ico* (2001) by Team Ico.

The Call-to-Action and Refusal of the Call

Another important consideration for storytelling in video games is the call-to-action—the event that sets dramatic events in motion. The call-to-action in video games comes in many forms: an opportunity to explore an inviting environment (curiosity); an immediate threat that must be neutralized or evaded (danger); or a quest to retrieve a special item (reward). A common occurrence in traditional story-telling is to have the protagonist refuse this initial call-to-action, such as Frodo's reluctance to guard the ring at the start of *The Lord of the Rings*. This *refusal of the call* is an important dramatic device because it raises tension for the impending story with a realistic reaction to life changing events—reflecting the protagonist's reluctance to leave the comfort and safety of his or her everyday existence.

Players of video games, however, revel in high-stakes action and behave more like the dwarf character, Gimli: "Certainty of death. Small chance of success. What are we waiting for?!" They do so because video games are forgiving compared to real life—allowing players to instantly replay difficult sections with minimum discomfort. *Tekken Torture Tournament* (2001), by Eddo Stern and Mark Allen, humorously spotlights the usual lack of empathy that players have toward their digital avatars by subjecting willing participants to bracing but non-lethal electric shocks in correspondence to injuries sustained by their in-game characters. As you can imagine, the threat of receiving an electric shock completely removes the usual sense of nonchalance while playing *Tekken 3* (1997), once the competitors' survival instincts kick in. Without such consequences, it's best to think of players as both a Guardian Angel and Devil's Advocate: somebody who wishes to safely guide their playable character through a narrative but is equally willing to take potentially fatal risks to overcome an obstacle or for curiosity's sake.

It is interesting to note that the refusal of call is easier to instigate in first-person games—and even more so in first-person virtual reality experiences—because the heightened sense of presence results in players feeling that they are personally vulnerable, not a character under their control.

Instant, Delayed, and Imagined Consequences

To counter the carefree attitude of players and induce a realistic sense of hesitation, it's important that gameplay includes lasting consequences. The Dark Souls series by FromSoftware, for instance, permanently confiscates hard-won items and points if players are unable to retrieve their corpse after dying in battle. This adds a tremendous amount of tension to each enemy encounter because players that build something up will consequently have something meaningful to lose. Alternatively, games like *Life Is Strange* (2015) by Dontnod Entertainment, and *The Walking Dead* series induce player hesitation by delaying the full repercussions of certain decisions until a few hours of gameplay have elapsed. Delaying the payoff—as opposed to giving instant feedback—makes it difficult for players to reverse earlier decisions and so they must carefully deliberate their options up-front, akin to the refusal of the call.

Survival horror games like the *Resident Evil* series (Figure 9.5) and the genre's pioneer, *Alone in the Dark* (1992), inspire a third approach, which is to activate

Figure 9.5 One of the most memorable gaming moments of all time occurs in *Resident Evil 2* (1998), by Capcom, is when players first glimpse a demonic-looking creature scurrying across the window toward the room that they must enter next, which leads players to approach every subsequent doorway with a sense of trepidation.

the player's imagination because it's much more vivid than anything the game can present. The latter, for instance, features an unavoidable trap in the game's first corridor that kills the player instantaneously. In fact, this is the only instance of such a trap in the entire game, which was deliberately planted by the game's designer, Frédérick Raynal, to put players ceaselessly on edge and on the lookout for danger perceived to be lurking at every turn.

Active Elements of Dynamic Composition

To help us align the elements of dynamic composition to the dramatic curve, it is helpful to use a *snapshot sequence* (Figure 9.6). The snapshot sequence is divided horizontally into columns, which reference the shape spectrum. The transition line marks the end of one gameplay segment and the beginning of a new one. The three empty columns are used to take a snapshot of dynamic composition at three important stages of a transition—relating to the call-to-action, anticipation, and contemplation. If at any time we wish to change the aesthetics of a particular moment, the elements of dynamic composition can be modified using the concepts explored in previous chapters. A three-point sequence helps maintain a simple orchestration of drama, while also ensuring that each aesthetic is distinct and clearly expressed. It becomes too difficult to discern state changes if there are too many gradations in the sequence.

Note that games won't always utilize all eight elements of dynamic composition. The state of dynamic composition elements can therefore be *active, inactive,*

		■ Theme1	● Theme2	▲ Theme3
☺	Character shapes and poses	Description	Description	Description
	Lines of movement			
	Environment shapes			
	Pathways			
	Dialogue			
	Framing			
	Audio			
	Player gestures		Transition	

Figure 9.6 The snapshot sequence table featuring the eight elements of dynamic composition in the left column, shape concepts and themes along the top row, and a transition line that marks adjoining gameplay segments.

or *absent*. What is important for drama, however, is that a minimum of two aesthetic states occur in sequence before the transition, as the dramatic experience will likely feel flat if only one shape concept is used to build tension. Designers will often designate one or two elements of dynamic composition to lead the drama, instead of using every element to its fullest.

Once the themes and active elements of dynamic composition have been identified, we can insert keywords in each row to describe the aesthetic state of each element. Keywords can be replaced or supplemented with sketches, concept images, and prototype screenshots. The order of shape concepts can also change depending on the requirements of the story. For instance, a transition could play out as either of the two sequences in Figure 9.7: triangle, circle, square to sequentially express aesthetic themes of pain, optimism, and loss (upper row); or circle, square, triangle to express themes of exploration, defense, and danger (lower row).

The snapshot sequence also allows us to consider core *game* mechanics versus core *aesthetic* mechanics. The distinction is important because core game

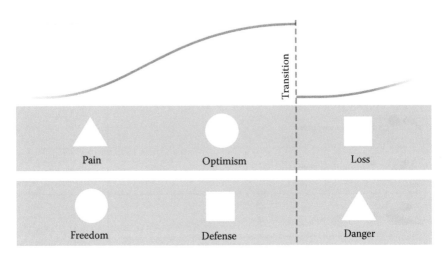

Figure 9.7 The sequence of shape concepts for a dramatic curve depends entirely on the needs of the story being told—hence the possibility to order the shape concepts in a multitude of ways and adapt their respective themes to the narrative.

mechanics define the player's principal abilities in the game, while core aesthetic mechanics have the strongest ability to shape the emotional experience of those abilities. For instance, the core game mechanic in a typical Mario game is *jumping*, which comes under lines of movement in the context of dynamic composition. The aesthetic experience of Mario's jump ability is modulated by environment shapes—in the form of ledges, pits, and enemy characters—which drastically change the aesthetic tension of the core game mechanic. Identifying the core aesthetic mechanic provides designers with the greatest fidelity to affect the player's gestures and modulate the narrative tension of a gameplay segment.

Mapping the Dramatic Curve

Once the active elements of dynamic composition have been identified and graded using a snapshot sequence table, we can go about mapping the themes onto a dramatic curve much like the previous example from *The Lord of the Rings: The Two Towers* in Section II (Figure SII.6). The major difference for a video game dramatic curve (Figure 9.8) is a second curve to indicate the flow of gameplay, and the primary shapes below the horizontal axis, which reference the aesthetic choices defined in the snapshot sequence. You may have noticed the dissonance between narrative and gameplay curves after the transition in Figure 9.8. This illustrates cases where noninteractive cutscenes are played and players can only watch passively without control over their in-game character. It is worth noting that the call-to-action and turning point for a video game transition is more effective if it involves player activity—as opposed to being presented via a cutscene or dialogue.

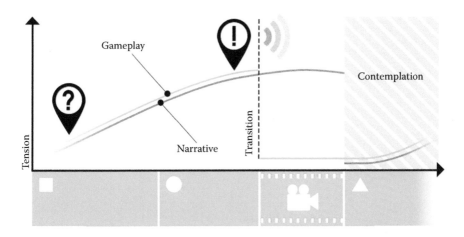

Figure 9.8 The dramatic curve for video games features the same basic functions as for film, with the exception of a second curve that indicates dramatic tension for interactivity, and pauses for noninteractive cutscenes, where applicable.

Summary

Player agency aside, the basic story structure of games mirrors that of films and literature too, in which transitions between levels, scenes, or chapters feature a call-to-action, turning point, contemplative space, and contrasting aesthetics. The major difference in video games is that during gameplay segments the player-audience guides the protagonist who must act against opposition to reach a goal that may, or may not, be resolved.

For video game storytelling to be as emotionally rich as possible, it is imperative that interaction and gameplay adhere to the fundamental design techniques perfected by traditional art and film. The following video game case studies bring together our accumulated knowledge of the shape spectrum and dynamic composition. These concepts collectively define video gaming's musical notes and musical chords, respectively, which are structured along the dramatic curve. We will use the dramatic curve to analyze video game transitions featuring sophisticated symphonies of interaction for which the player acts as conductor.

So, how are the concepts of anticipation, contemplation, and contrast from film transitions reflected in some of the most highly rated video games from recent years? We'll explore this question in the following chapter by applying the concepts to a series of case studies of award-winning games.

10 Transitions with Cutscenes

In this chapter we will explore the orchestration of transitions along the dramatic curve in games that prominently feature cutscenes to propel the story. Cutscenes are predefined, noninteractive events that use cinematic storytelling techniques to set the stage for subsequent gameplay (see Chapter 5, Cutscene Prompts section) and introduce dramatic subtext, which is usually too subtle to convey during gameplay (refer to Chapter 7, the Overt Drama versus Subtext section). The cinematic quality of cutscenes means that they offer designers an easy way to string together interactive segments of gameplay using familiar filmic techniques. For our purposes, transitions with cutscenes are an excellent starting point for the adaption of the techniques introduced with *The Lord of the Rings: The Two Towers* transition in Section II.

The artistic versatility of primary shapes—the circle, square, and triangle—and their associated themes will become apparent as we analyze the dramatic events for each video game example below. The analyses will be used to complete a snapshot sequence for each game, which is subsequently mapped to a dramatic curve. This is only the first step to developing an appreciation for the interconnectedness between storytelling across all game development disciplines, so that we are collectively aware of the fundamental techniques necessary to deliver gaming experiences that promote emotions and story clarity. The first game to be studied is the award-winning title, *The Last of Us: Left Behind* (2014)—the downloadable sequel to *The Last of Us* by California-based developer Naughty Dog.

Case Study: *The Last of Us: Left Behind*

Developer: Naughty Dog
Video search term: "The Last of Us Left Behind Chapter 3 So Close"

The call-to-action that defines the player's goal and the lever of tension for gameplay is communicated in the opening cutscene of *The Last of Us: Left Behind*. The player learns that Ellie must retrieve a health pack to heal her injured friend and fellow survivor, Joel.

Drama Analysis

The drama in Figure 10.1 from "Chapter 3: So Close" is set in a desolate mall. The playable character, Ellie, must retrieve a health pack from a crashed helicopter precariously perched on an overhead ledge (Figure 10.1a), which invites the player to tilt the camera upward for an imposing high-angle perspective of the objective. The player must first explore the surrounding environment in search of a way to unlock the gate leading to the upper floor (Figure 10.1b) before negotiating the Clicker enemies patrolling the courtyard directly below the helicopter (Figure 10.1c). In the final approach to the helicopter, Ellie ascends a fragile ledge, forcing the player to proceed tentatively so as not to shatter the glass underfoot (Figure 10.1d). This segment is framed with an overhead camera that emphasizes Ellie's vulnerability and the elevation of the platform. The end of the platform features a narrow, angled turn, at the end of which a final jump must be performed to reach the crashed helicopter without falling to the Clicker-infested grounds below (Figure 10.1e). At this point, an animated cutscene is automatically played, in which the turning point sees Ellie huddling with the sought after health pack and twice affirm to herself: "I'm not letting you go, I'm not letting you go" (Figure 10.1f). After the transition and just before gameplay resumes, the narrative crosscuts to a new scene that shows Ellie reunited with her friend, Riley, as they open a door (Figure 10.1g) to reveal an inviting and warm environment that the player is free to explore at their own pace (Figure 10.1h)—followed by a camera that is aligned to Ellie's eye-level.

To show something for what it truly is, it is essential to contrast it with what it isn't. Without experiencing what loneliness is through Ellie's eyes we could not hope to know what togetherness feels like either. The gameplay transition achieves a heartbreaking sense of loneliness primarily due to the powerful contrast of aesthetics—fear and loneliness versus safety and togetherness—elicited between the snow-infested mall (Figure 10.1a–f) and the warmth of the fairground carousel (Figure 10.1h).

Snapshot Sequence

The snapshot sequence in Figure 10.2 illustrates the key elements of dynamic composition that are used to orchestrate the majority of transitions in *The Last of Us* series. Note how gameplay illustrated in Figure 10.1a–e of the transition features explorative or aggressive aesthetic themes—such as stealth walking, narrow uphill pathways and enemy secondary characters. After the

Figure 10.1 The above transition from *The Last of Us: Left Behind* (2014), by Naughty Dog, demonstrates a sophisticated level of orchestration that dramatically contrasts the aesthetics of a desolate mall with a flashback to a more tender moment in the protagonist's past.

transition—from Figure 10.1h and beyond—the same elements of dynamic composition reflect a playful theme. During these latter instances, no immediate action is required, thus providing the player with a quiet space in which to engage in deductive reasoning and contemplate "What is it that Ellie does not wish to let go?"

The core game mechanic in *The Last of Us* series is *stealth-survival*, as players must traverse perilous environments with considered use of weaponry and tactical use of the environment. The *core aesthetic mechanic*—the element of dynamic composition with the greatest ability to influence the aesthetic experience of

		Exploration	Danger	Play
☺	Character shapes and poses	Neutral	Stealth and fighting pose	Upbeat
�	Lines of movement	Purposeful	Running and hiding	Playful
▲▲	Environment shapes	Square shapes	Angular shapes and enemy characters	Round shapes and friendly characters
⌇	Pathways	Straight and wide	Angular and narrow pathways, and locked doors	Curved or "open canvas"
💬	Dialogue	Alone	Enemy takedowns	Harmonious
▭	Framing	Level	Upwards	Level
♪	Audio	Ominous ambient sounds	Screeching of enemies	Tender melody
🖐	Player gestures	Controlled, purposeful	Aggressive or restless	Casual, relaxed

Transition

Figure 10.2 Once the drama has been analyzed, a sequence of shape concepts is determined and inserted into the snapshot sequence so that each element of dynamic composition can be graded in the context of the corresponding themes.

stealth-survival—is modulated by the environment and pathways in the form of enemies and locked doors.

Mapping the Dramatic Curve

Once the active elements of dynamic composition have been identified and their tension graded with a snapshot sequence, we can go about mapping the elements to a dramatic curve that includes narrative *and* gameplay threads (Figure 10.3). Storytelling in video games is at its best when the player's agency is in harmony with the predefined narrative designed by the game's development team.

Attention Bottleneck

Adding gameplay to the dramatic curve highlights a complication especially prevalent in video games: *attention bottleneck*. Attention bottleneck refers to the phenomenon of overloading the audience with too much information. Giving players too much to simultaneously see and do reduces their ability to contemplate and emotionally engage with the story. This extends to cutscenes, which are

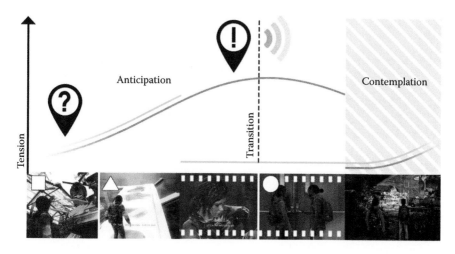

Figure 10.3 The shape concepts summarized in the snapshot sequence above are mapped to the dramatic curve, which locates the call-to-action and turning point, and visualizes the moment of contemplation and emotional echo (noting that gameplay stops during noninteractive cutscenes).

noninteractive because gameplay is halted but nonetheless demand a certain level of concentration from the player.

The moment of contemplation in video games must therefore be treated with even more respect and sensitivity than with film.

The ideal solution is to completely remove the need for the player to act immediately following the transition, to the extent that players could conceivably put their game controller down without suffering any consequences. Which is exactly what happens in the transition from *The Last of Us: Left Behind*, in which all the elements of dynamic composition are set to a low-tension state following the cutscene—allowing the player to contemplate the unfortunate circumstances of the friendship between Ellie and her best friend, Riley. The key takeaway here is that the player is physically experiencing the narrative through gestures on the game controller in response to on-screen events (do, don't show).

Attention bottleneck is even more detrimental to the story if the player is not able to retain an overview of the larger context of their actions. Because gameplay demands such a high level of cognitive engagement, players quickly forget the overarching context of their actions in the game. The player's context is easier to reiterate when the game's environment is located aboveground because prominent landmarks can be placed along the skyline (Figure 10.4a). In enclosed spaces—such as building interiors or below ground—it is significantly more difficult for players to maintain a macro perspective of the story (Figure 10.4b). The consequence can be a purely egocentric narrative, where players become solely preoccupied with short-term obstacles in their immediate path.

The difficulty developers therefore face is finding the right balance between calling attention to the larger narrative and allowing players to focus on their own unique experiences. The perfect balance creates a space in which the

(a)   (b)

Figure 10.4 Prominent landmarks, such as the bridge (a) in *The Last of Us* series, by Naughty Dog, help to orientate the player within the game's narrative, while the restricted light of the torch beam (b) illustrates the phenomenon of attention bottleneck that reduces the player's awareness of the game's overarching narrative.

player's actions and personal experiences feel like they have a greater, more epic meaning within the game's make-believe universe. Attention bottleneck is a significant issue for game design and the reason why this topic has been allocated its own chapter titled Reiteration of Themes and Gameplay Objectives (Chapter 11).

Let's try our hand at two other video game transitions with cutscenes—starting with the sensitive storytelling in *Brothers: A Tale of Two Sons* (2013), by Swedish developer Starbreeze Studio. The following analysis comes with a spoiler alert!

Case Study: *Brothers: A Tale of Two Sons*

Brothers: A Tale of Two Sons is another game that uses cutscenes to convey dramatic context and mood for segments of gameplay. The game is the result of a collaboration between Starbreeze Studios and award-winning Swedish film director, Josef Fares.

Developer: Starbreeze Studios
Video search term: "Brothers A Tale Of Two Sons Ending"

Drama Analysis

The gameplay sequence begins with the player simultaneously controlling the two brothers, Naiee and Naia, moments after the sequence's call-to-action that sees the elder brother, Naia, mortally wounded during an encounter with a spider creature (Figure 10.5). Naiee and Naia's combined movements are strained and erratic because of Naia's injury (Figure 10.5a). A sudden rockslide sends them sliding down a chute (Figure 10.5b) that fortuitously brings them to the Tree of Life—the overarching goal of their journey—from which the brothers wish to collect healing water for their ailing father back home. The healthy Naiee is instructed by his elder brother to make the last ascent alone. With a renewed pace and a sense of optimism, the player controls the single figure of Naiee as he ascends the mystical

Figure 10.5 The above transition from *Brothers: A Tale of Two Sons* (2013), by Starbreeze Studios, uses optimism to create tension, which is contrasted by the tragic event that occurs after the transition.

tree (Figure 10.5c) to collect the elixir (Figure 10.5d). The turning point occurs when he returns to his brother to find that Naia has passed away (Figure 10.5e)—conveyed through a noninteractive cutscene. After the cutscene—once gameplay resumes—the player controls a slow and visibly grieving Naiee, who must bury his deceased brother (Figure 10.5f).

Snapshot Sequence

When we collate the active elements of dynamic composition for the transition in *Brothers: A Tale of Two Sons*, we find that it has been orchestrated using a different sequence of shape concepts to that of *The Last of Us: Left Behind*. The aesthetic theme for each shape concept has been adjusted to the requirements of this particular story—triangle/pain, circle/positivity, and square/loss—while still aligning to the general aesthetic characteristics of each shape (Figure 10.6), which we explored in Section I.

The core game mechanic of *Brothers: A Tale of Two Sons* is *traversal*—much like in *The Last of Us* series. Although here the core aesthetic mechanism is greatly affected by moments when players must control both Naiee and Naia

		Pain ▲	Optimism ●	Loss ■
😃	Character shapes and poses	Strained, injured	Energetic	Grieving
➜●	Lines of movement	Erratic (both brothers)	Fast (Naiee, only)	Lethargic (Naiee, only)
〜	Pathways	Angular	Curved	Linear
▲▲	Environment shapes	Hard	Organic	Vertical
♪	Audio	Wind and crashing boulders	Uplifting melody	Long, arresting notes
↻	Player gestures	Erratic	Casual, relaxed	Slow, deliberate

Figure 10.6 The snapshot sequence for *Brothers: A Tale of Two Sons* serves as a summary for the transition's dramatic structure, and reveals a triangle-circle-square sequence of shape concepts to respectively transport themes of pain, optimism, and loss.

simultaneously versus low-tension moments when each brother can be controlled individually. Therefore, both the core game mechanic and core aesthetic mechanic come under lines of movement.

Mapping the Dramatic Curve

The dramatic curve for *Brother: A Tale of Two Sons* (Figure 10.7) further reveals how the transition's heartbreaking sense of loss is generated. The narrative and gameplay misdirect the player toward feelings of optimism generated by setting a clear goal (reach the top of the tree and the elixir of life) along a singular path with a quickness of pace added to the playable character. This sense of optimism, heightened by an uplifting melody, makes the tragic turn of events even more powerful after the transition. This is a great example of alternative methods for generating narrative tension to the confrontational end-of-level boss battles typical of most video games. As with *The Last of Us: Left Behind*, true contemplation happens only after the cutscene has finished (Figure 10.5f). At this point, the player does not have any pressing tasks to perform and is free to pause activity for as long as he or she wishes. The shape concepts underline the key aesthetic message: where life equals movement (circle), death equals stillness (square). The

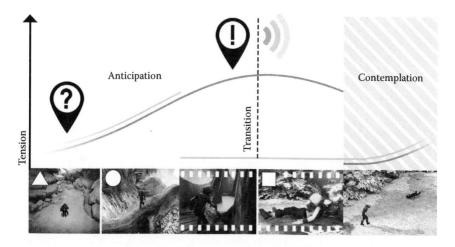

Figure 10.7 The dramatic curve structures the gameplay analysis and snapshot sequence so that we can appreciate the wider context of the call-to-action, turning point, and moment of contemplation across the transition.

sense of loss is made more emotionally poignant through the game's ability to elicit the corresponding physical gestures in the player.

The following case study from *Portal 2* (2011), by Valve, demonstrates further versatility of our primary shapes, and the shape spectrum in orchestrating video game transitions.

Case Study: *Portal 2*

Portal 2 features a sophisticated story and clever wit delivered by the game's rivaling antagonists, Wheatley and GLaDOS. *Portal 2*'s game mechanics refreshingly avoid aggressive conflict, so that tension is generated using alternative means. The game's designers achieve this splendidly by twisting the environment into emotionally charged forms, which our shape spectrum lens can effectively reveal.

Developer: Valve
Video search term: "Portal 2 GLaDOS Awakens"

Drama Analysis

In the opening sequence of *Portal 2* the player is woken from stasis and must perform a series of spatial puzzles while maneuvering weighted cubes to switches that open doors (Figure 10.8a). Along the way they are guided by the blundering Wheatley (Figure 10.8b,c), who tries to help players escape the science facility while circumventing the lifeless robotic body of GLaDOS (Figure 10.8d)—an artificially intelligent computer system that was killed by the protagonist, Chell,

Figure 10.8 Guided by the witty ramblings of Wheatley, this transition from *Portal 2* (2011) by Valve, directs players through an environment that gradually twists and fractures to transmit a sense of impending trouble.

in the game's prequel. The call-to-action that levers tension for this gameplay segment is the question of whether the player and Wheatley will make it past GLaDOS safely. Wheatley crushes hopes of escape by inadvertently reactivating GLaDOS (Figure 10.8e) at the turning point—an event played out via a semi-interactive cutscene. The newly awakened GLaDOS (Figure 10.8f), simmering with resentment, throws the player down a garbage chute to the sounds of crashing machinery (Figure 10.8g) into the depths of the incinerator room (Figure 10.8h) where gameplay resumes.

Snapshot Sequence

As mentioned in the closing paragraphs of Chapter 8, it is not essential that a game's shape concepts neatly align with the circle, square, or triangle. What is important is that primary shapes and the shape spectrum underline the importance of having a range of visually distinct and aesthetically differing shapes embedded in a sequence to create emotionally rich transitions—as exemplified by the snapshot sequence for *Portal 2* in Figure 10.9.

The square-shaped test chambers of *Portal 2* provide the objective environment in which puzzles must be solved, while circular portals, doorways, and switches indicate escape routes—a concept underscored in the breadcrumb trail illustration of dots illuminated on the chamber walls (Figure 10.8a). The regularity of the test facility (Figure 10.8b) begins to twist and turn (Figure 10.8c) as the player approaches the inactive body of GLaDOS—creating a visual imbalance that foreshadows the upcoming confrontation with the game's deranged antagonist. GLaDOS is represented by a spiral, or broken circle (Figure 10.8c and d), which is a shape concept with symbolic connotations concerning the player's state of affairs and the mental condition of GLaDOS. The player is then directed to descend a series of steps and ledges (echoing the concepts that we explored in the Creating Layers of Emotions with Camera Angles section in Chapter 6) where the spiral placement of switches viewed from the base of the main breaker room (Figure 10.8e) further foreshadow the unexpected reactivation of GLaDOS. The player is implicitly directed to tilt the camera downward when GLaDOS is inactive (Figure 10.8d) and upward when she is reactivated (Figure 10.8f), which diminishes and boosts her status, respectively.

	Objectivity	Insanity	Danger
Pathways	Straight	Side-to-side	Angular
Environment shapes	Perpendicular	Spiraling	Angular
Framing	Upward	Downward	Level
Audio	Ominous sound effects and white noise	Ominous music	Crashing heavy industrial machinery
Player gestures	Direct	Swerving	Hesitant

Figure 10.9 *Portal 2*'s snapshot sequence clarifies the game's sophisticated shape concepts, which immerse players in a thematic sequence of objectivity, insanity, and danger.

In terms of character-environment shape relationships discussed in Chapter 3, the broken circle of GLaDOS' design is mirrored in her surroundings—visually communicating that the player has stepped into her deranged world (Figure 10.8f). The player's plunging descent down the garbage chute reintroduces the objective square shape concept of the test chambers, with the addition of spiked garbage crushers (Figure 10.8g) that set the emotional stage of gameplay that follows—void of circular-shaped escape routes (Figure 10.8h).

Portal 2's core gameplay mechanic is *navigation*, which involves firing a portal gun to create pathways combined with platform-jumping elements. What is particularly interesting about the transition is that it does not feature any of *Portal 2*'s core gameplay. Therefore, tension is generated through aesthetics and not escalating puzzle difficulty—as would be the norm. Instead, this universally acclaimed game uses a dramatic shape system to tell its story of comic tragedy. From the previous snapshot sequence we can deduce that the shape of pathways defines the sequence's core aesthetic mechanic.

Mapping the Dramatic Curve

The dramatic curve for this gameplay sequence in *Portal 2* affirms the sophisticated orchestration of shape concepts across the transition (Figure 10.10). Once gameplay resumes after the transition cutscene, the player is given time to contemplate events because no immediate action is required. They could conceivably put the controller down without suffering any consequences. The inversion of aesthetics—from a day-lit, semi-organic setting to the bone-crushing industrial belly of the incinerator room—allow the player to feel the emotional echo from their intimidating first encounter with GLaDOS.

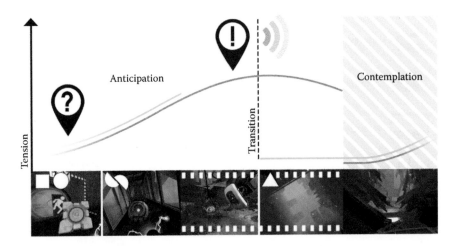

Figure 10.10 The dramatic curve gives us a high-level overview of how *Portal 2*'s grand exposition has been orchestrated to consider gameplay using pathways in the environment to shape the player's progress in the lead-up to the dramatic encounter with GLaDOS.

Replay

A genre that we've not yet explored in this chapter concerns episodic games such as, *The Walking Dead* (2012) and *Life is Strange* (2015). Now that you're versed in the fundamental techniques of transitions in video games, take some time out to play through your favorite episodic game. Create a snapshot sequence of dynamic composition and map it to the dramatic curve—searching in particular for the call-to-action, turning point, and the moment of contemplation and emotional echo. What you'll find particular to episodic games is that each episode tends to end in a dramatic cliffhanger, which leaves players reeling as the credits role—anxiously awaiting a continuation of the story in the vacuum of what would otherwise be the beginning of the subsequent gameplay sequence.

For example, at the end of season 2, episode 5 of *The Walking Dead* video game series developed by Telltale Games, players can witness one of several endings in which the young Clementine is seen walking with baby Alvin Jr. (AJ) in her arms toward a herd of zombie walkers. She stops to finish off an injured walker and covers herself and AJ in its guts—presumably allowing the two to safely pass through the herd undetected. However, the episode ends with a sudden cut to black before players can discover whether Clementine's daring strategy was successful (Figure 10.11).

Figure 10.11 The ending of *The Walking Dead: Season 2, Episode 5: No Going Back* (2012) by Telltale Games, demonstrates a technique often employed in episodic titles where the game ends just before a particularly dramatic turning point—emotionally hooking players to anxiously await the next episode when the outcome of a character's action promises to be revealed.

Transitions and Cutscene Alignment

The inclusion of cutscenes in video games brings up another storytelling consideration: to which side of the transition does a cutscene belong? Due to their non-interactive nature, cutscenes are conceptually no different to the medium of film and are consequently heavily used in narrative-driven games like *The Last of Us*, *Tomb Raider*, and *Mass Effect*, which aim to create a cinematic, character-driven experience. The ideal is that cutscenes should be fluid and continuous with the in-game narrative. You may have noticed that the cutscenes from *The Last of Us: Left Behind*, *Brothers: A Tale of Two Sons*, and *Portal 2* straddle the transition line—although this is not always the case.

Cutscenes can also be placed before the transition and after the transition and at any time during gameplay whenever subtext or subtle storytelling must be conveyed. Knowing that events immediately before the transition are activity-orientated and events immediately after the transition are contemplation-orientated will determine the content of the cutscene. In general, the shorter and quieter the cutscene after the transition the better—as we saw in the moment of Legolas' contemplative whisper from *The Lord of the Rings: The Two Towers* (Figure SII.5)—while cutscenes before the transition can be dynamic and eventful.

Summary

Cutscenes bring interactivity to a dramatic stop, allowing designers to convey subtle elements of a story and spotlight important events that may otherwise be overlooked during gameplay. The above case studies exemplify the most effective use of cutscenes, which serve to support the dramatic curve and ensure that the flow between gameplay is as fluid as possible. Rather than set forward simple exposition, the content of a cutscene should ideally engage the imagination of players and give them interesting narrative questions to contemplate. Cutscenes are best restricted to a short duration because players prefer to get on with interactivity and gameplay.

To help study and orchestrate emotionally rich transitions in games it is beneficial to use the dynamic composition framework, which combines the primary shape concepts, the dramatic curve and transition techniques. Such a structured approach is extremely empowering because it's akin to plucking the strings of an instrument and having a clear and unified idea of what effect it will have on the player-audience. In the following chapter, we will explore the aforementioned process of reiterating the context of the story, which is an essential yet often undervalued component of storytelling in games.

⑪ Reiteration of Themes and Gameplay Objectives

In the previous chapter, we explored transition techniques in video games to understand the importance of aesthetic clarity and contrast for amplifying emotional experiences and story. The process highlighted that gaming's added element of interactivity creates significant problems concerning attention bottleneck, and how much information players can mentally process at any one time. Attention bottleneck is also a concern for film directors who counteract the phenomenon with a continuous reiteration of vital story information as it begins to fade from the audience's mind. Legendary illustrator and storyteller, Iain McCaig—who is credited as a concept artist on illustrious films like *The Terminator 2: Judgment Day* (1991) and *Star Wars: The Force Awakens* (2015)—describes the reiteration process by framing it from the audience's perspective and its story-orientation needs from moment to moment:

"Where are we?
"Who are we?
"What are we talking about?
"Where are we again?"

Where, Who, What, and (Again) Where…

Iain McCaig's quote is illustrated by the sequence of stills from *Star Wars Episode IV: A New Hope* (1977) (Figure 11.1), in which a long-shot establishes where the forthcoming action will take place (Where are we?). The audience is then presented with a medium-shot highlighting the figures that are the primary subject of the scene (Who are we?). A close-up finally addresses the details of the

Figure 11.1 *Star Wars Episode IV: A New Hope* (1977), Lucasfilm Ltd., directed by George Lucas. The above shot sequence illustrates how film directors tackle attention bottleneck by presenting audiences with a cycling sequence of shots that continually reiterate the action from three different zoom levels.

scene (what are we talking about?). This cycle of long-medium-close-up shots is repeated as often as is necessary, whenever the director and film editor sense that key story information may be fading from the audience's memory (where are we again?).

The first scene, which follows the heroes, is contrasted by a switch in focus to the antagonist in the next scene, and so on (Figure 11.2). This back-and-forth between the protagonists and antagonists further reiterates the major conflicts within the story.

Reiteration of overarching narrative information that is critical to the effectiveness of a story is equally important in video games as it is in film. However, reiteration is not easily managed in games because interaction demands such a high level of cognitive engagement that the player's awareness of vital story

Figure 11.2 *Star Wars Episode IV: A New Hope* (1977), Lucasfilm Ltd., directed by George Lucas. The action in *A New Hope* continually jumps between the protagonists and antagonists—ensuring the audience does not forget the overarching conflict of the film.

information fades even quicker in the midst of gameplay. The result is the aforementioned egocentric narrative, where players become solely concerned with whatever obstacles happen to be placed in their immediate path. Game designers must therefore continually reiterate themes and gameplay objectives through local and global story cues that prevent players from (metaphorically speaking) looking down at their feet for too long. These cues should ideally be communicated within the story world, as opposed to externally in the form of stats and objectives listed in menus and the user interface. Failing to reiterate important information will result in players forgetting the call-to-action and the purpose of gameplay—invalidating the larger narrative that designers likely spent months or years carefully crafting.

Local Points of Interest

On a micro level, the playable character's gaze can reiterate gameplay objectives by directing players to points of interest, such as in *Uncharted 3: Drake's Deception*, where Nathan Drake's gaze acts like an arrow that directs attention to objects in the environment that may be of relevance. The screenshot in Figure 11.3 illustrates such a situation in Chapter 2: Greatness from Small Beginnings where players must search a museum exhibit to find Sir Francis Drake's ring.

The more embedded the story cues within the game world, the more effective they will be at reiterating context while maintaining the player's sense of immersion. For example, Nathan's gaze is accompanied by an audible inner dialogue that reiterates the context of the player's actions while gameplay can continue unhindered. Sidekicks like Riley in *The Last of Us: Left Behind*, and Wheatley and GLaDOS in *Portal 2* also serve as reiteration devices. A simpler alternative is to use audio diaries that are played via a menu or written memos that the player must read—although the latter device breaks the flow of gameplay.

Another approach to reiterate narrative themes on a local level is to use an item loaded with emotional value—the mere sight of which prompts players to reflect on the overarching story. It's important that such a visual refrain is presented in moderation: not too often to avoid diluting its value, and just enough to prevent it slipping from the player's mind altogether. *Firewatch* (2016), by Campo Santo, uses such an item in the form of the protagonist's wedding ring, which serves to remind players of the game's tragic exposition and the theme of memory. The protagonist's wedding ring remains off-screen for much of the game and appears mostly when the protagonist, Henry, is climbing up rocks and the view is conveniently focused on his hands. Players have a few opportunities to interact with the ring after they find it placed on the desk in Henry's lookout tower (Figure 11.4).

Figure 11.3 *Uncharted 3: Drake's Deception* (2011), by Naughty Dog, uses the playable character's gaze to direct players toward points of interest.

Figure 11.4 Henry, the playable character in *Firewatch* (2016), by Campo Santo, wears a wedding ring that functions as a visual refrain to remind players of the heartrending events that drove him to become a fire lookout.

This interaction is important because it revives the emotional value and narrative theme associated with the ring—whether or not players choose to replace it on the protagonist's finger.

Planting Narrative Cues

The ideal is that the reiteration of narrative themes and gameplay objectives is presented visually within the game world in a way that players feels like they alone discovered the cue, even when the game's designers deliberately inserted it. *Brothers: A Tale of Two Sons* features a fictional language, which required the developers to convey the story through character gestures and visual cues within the game world. During the game, players discover several successive instances of foreshadowing when accompanying their mysterious female companion. In the first instance (Figure 11.5a), the long-abandoned boat implies previous visitors. A second instance is communicated through the manner in which the female crawls, spider-like, across the fallen tree foreshadowing the conflict near the end of the game (Figure 11.5b). The third instance (Figure 11.5c) is more explicit—when the group encounters a frozen army at the gates of an old town. The visual cue serves to prime players for the upcoming encounter and consider the worst possible outcome.

In film production this particular technique is called *planting*, which refers to the seemingly casual presentation of an object or information that the player-audience can later recall when it takes on a central role in the narrative. The technique serves the purpose of concealing an instance of deus ex machina by planting a gameplay solution in advance of an event—rather than the answer

Figure 11.5 The seemingly innocuous planting of narrative cues in *Brothers: A Tale of Two Sons* (2013) by Starbreeze Studios, means that players feel a greater sense of ownership in piecing together the narrative—such as the abandoned boat (a), the spidery gestures of the female companion (b), and the frozen army of human statues (c), which later become essential to progress (d).

conveniently presenting itself at just the moment when it is needed. The payoff in this example is when players discover that they can hide behind the frozen human statues to avoid being spotted by the invisible monster (Figure 11.5d).

Reiteration of Setting

Before the player becomes too engrossed in gameplay within their immediate surroundings, it is helpful to employ cinematic long-shots to reiterate the context of where the action is taking place. Developer Naughty Dog uses this technique throughout *Uncharted 3: Drake's Deception* (2011) to communicate the setting and scale of the drama in Chapter 14: Cruisin' for a Bruisin' and Chapter 15: Sink or Swim (Figure 11.6). Long-shots are presented on several occasions in-between protracted periods of close-up action. Each time a long-shot is presented to set the stage of action, the camera is subsequently zoomed in to reveal a vulnerable-looking Nathan Drake, who the player must guide to safety. The dynamic zooming in works to reiterate the drama in this example because the level design easily allows the camera to pull out to frame the exterior of the ship. But once the player enters the ship's interior, reiterating the setting of the story becomes significantly harder.

Figure 11.6 *Uncharted 3: Drake's Deception* (2011), by Naughty Dog, uses a similar device to that of the *Star Wars* sequence of stills, in which the camera is frequently zoomed in and out to reiterate the wider circumstances in which the action is taking place.

Reiterating the Call-to-Action

Interior environments cause a particular problem for reiterating gameplay objectives because the enclosed space prevents the in-game camera from zooming in and out on the action. As a consequence, the player's awareness of the primary objective for a particular level can begin to fade. In Figure 11.7 from *The Last of Us* (2013), by Naughty Dog, the player must navigate the sewers to reach the radio tower located aboveground on the other side. The context of the player's actions—to escape the sewers and reach relative safety—is presented at several points in the level. It's important to note that due to attention bottleneck players are often so distracted by gameplay that they often overlook the significance of these glimpses to the outside world, which serve to emotionally reiterate their goal. Players instead concern themselves with locating the next puzzle to solve—such as reaching the electric generator, killing a group of enemies, or locating hidden ammunition—without bothering to look up to appreciate the view once they determine that it's not the official path of escape.

Hence, a careful balance must be struck between luring players into thinking that such reiteration devices represent genuine opportunities for interaction or highlight their perfunctory value up-front to avoid unsuspecting players wasting their time trying to find a non-existent solution to progress.

Figure 11.7 *The Last of Us* (2013), by Naughty Dog, continually reiterates the player's call-to-action through level design—such as the ceiling openings scattered throughout the sewers in Chapter 6: The Suburbs, which deliberately give players false hope of immediate escape but ultimately serve only to remind them of their goal.

Reiteration of Global Objectives

Another approach to global reiteration of gameplay objectives is the placement of prominent landmarks within the video game environment. When players lose their way exploring the uninhabited Hebridean landscape of *Dear Esther* (2012), by The Chinese Room, they are promptly reminded of their final destination by the ominously flashing red light atop the radio mast, which is visible from most locations on the island (Figure 11.8). The radio mast functions much like the mysterious mountain in *Journey*, by thatgamecompany, which serves to orientate players and provide clear global objectives.

Figure 11.8 *Dear Esther* (2012) by The Chinese Room uses a technique of guiding players through open environments using a prominent landmark that can be seen from almost every location in the game.

Orientation

The general trend in story-driven video games is toward environments with an endlessly changing sequence of locations, which make it difficult for players to maintain a mental map of the game environment. In contrast, smaller environments work hand-in-hand with prominent landmarks to reiterate the overarching narrative and player objectives. A great example is Yamatai Island, the setting for *Tomb Raider* (2013), which helps players maintain a mental map of events by having them revisit the same locations at different points in the game as well as presenting prominent landmarks visible from various vantage points on the island (Figure 11.9).

Revisiting locations is an important device for reiterating narrative themes in open-world games, where many overlapping story threads can be active at the same time. Rather than allow scripted story events to occur anywhere within the game world, designers preselect a limited number of locations—such as Grove Street, featured in *Grand Theft Auto IV* and *Grand Theft Auto V*—which develop layers of special meaning through repeat visits by players over the course of a game or series (Figure 11.10). Whenever the narrative requires that players remember an event that may have occurred many gameplay hours beforehand, designers can plant a checkpoint at one of these select locations to refresh the player's memory. Upon arriving, automated dialogue and behavior from nonplayable characters can further remind players of previous events and the context of the current situation.

Figure 11.9 The modestly sized setting of *Tomb Raider* (2013), by Crystal Dynamics, demonstrates the advantages of having players revisit locations to create stronger mental maps of the game's narrative and environment.

(a)   (b)

Figure 11.10 Locations can develop significant emotional value if they are repeatedly used as a setting for important narrative events—such as Grove Street in (a) *Grand Theft Auto IV* (2008) and (b) *Grand Theft Auto V* (2013) by Rockstar North.

Dual Perspectives with Nested Frames

For an even broader and versatile reiteration of story context we can seek inspiration from Quantic Dream's, *Fahrenheit* (known as *Indigo Prophecy* in North America). The game uses a device in which the visual frame is split for the narrative purpose of showing two different events occurring at the same moment. One of the panels remains dedicated to gameplay and under the player's control. The second panel, known as a *nested frame*, is noninteractive and can be used to inform the player of immediate or distant events occurring away from the player's immediate location.

Figure 11.11 features a moment from Fahrenheit in which the main protagonist and culprit, Lucas Kane, is paid a visit by police lieutenant, Carla Valenti. The

Figure 11.11 *Fahrenheit* (2005), by Quantic Dream, raises dramatic tension with nested frames that show two different events occurring simultaneously—such as the impending arrival of a police officer (lower frame) at the playable character's office (upper frame).

Figure 11.12 In this example from *Valiant Hearts: The Great War* (2014), by Ubisoft, the left frame is where gameplay occurs while the nested frame on the right cuts away to pertinent events that would otherwise be out of view.

player must conceal incriminating evidence before Carla reaches his office. The impending moment is dramatically visualized by Carla's approaching footsteps in the lower, nested panel.

A similar approach to *Fahrenheit*'s is evidenced in *Valiant Hearts: The Great War* (2014), by developer Ubisoft Montpellier, in which noninteractive comic-style panels are nested in the larger frame without causing interruption to game-play. The effect is that players can witness the wider context of their actions while remaining engaged in their current activity (Figure 11.12).

Reiteration of Previous Events

Just as important as guiding players to up-coming objectives is having players look back and reflect on previous events. *The Witcher 3: Wild Hunt* (2015), by Polish developer CD Projekt RED, packs over 100 hours of unique gameplay time. To ensure that important events are kept fresh and emotionally meaning-ful, the game employs flashback cinematics whenever the game is started, which summarizes key events experienced during the player's previous play sessions (Figure 11.13). A more practical quest journal is also featured in the user interface where players can review their progress in the game. The game's advanced narra-tive system means that the repercussions of a player's action may become appar-ent after 5 hours plus of play time. To make the repercussions meaningful, quest designers regularly direct players to revisit familiar locations, and use dialogue from nonplayable characters to reiterate the player's previous actions.

Figure 11.13 *The Witcher 3: Wild Hunt* (2015), by CD Projekt RED, uses comic book style flashbacks to remind players of previous events each time they load the game.

Multiple Narrative Perspectives

More importantly, *The Witcher 3: Wild Hunt* features what is arguably the most exciting and little-explored avenue for reiterating narrative themes and gameplay objectives: the game allows players to experience the narrative from the perspective of two different protagonists—Geralt, and Ciri—which is an approach pioneered by games like *Halo 2* (2004) by Bungie (Figure 11.14).

Halo 2 allows players to experience two sides of a conflict through gameplay, by allowing them to take control of both Master Chief and the Arbiter—a member of the Covenant Elite enemy—at different points in the narrative. Allowing

Figure 11.14 *Halo 2* (2004) by Bungie is one of a few games that deliver emotional complexity by allowing players to take control of characters on both sides of the narrative conflict.

players such an opportunity underpins the motto of "do, don't show," because shifting between two playable characters within one game opens up opportunities for players to experience two very distinct aesthetics. Alternatively, the narrative can also allow players to experience the same character at different stages in their life, as in *Uncharted 4*, by Naughty Dog, which explores the protagonist's experiences as a child and adult.

Summary

There are certainly many more solutions for reiterating context waiting to be discovered. The future of storytelling in video games will demand increasingly more sophisticated and varied reiteration devices that don't resort to cutscenes so that gameplay can continue unhindered. Without such techniques players can only blindly follow events presented to them without having a global appreciation for the context of their actions. As we learned from *The Lord of the Rings*: *The Two Towers* example in Section II, a good story allows its audience to draw its own story conclusions under the watchful eye of the film director (or game design team).

We now have a solid understanding of transitions in games featuring cutscenes, and the importance of reiterating context. Before we begin exploring advanced transition techniques in games without cutscenes and open-world games, we must examine the various design pitfalls that can break the effectiveness of a carefully orchestrated video game transition.

 # Transition Hazards

Orchestrating an emotionally rich video game transition is an extremely complex task that requires the whole development team work closely together so that each element of the game is in tune with the same aesthetic goals. The following examples will help development teams save valuable time and money by highlighting common transition mishaps that can damage the effectiveness of a transition.

Interrupted Transitions

Transitions should be handled with extreme respect because they constitute the storytelling pillars of a narrative—the narrative points at which important story information is disclosed and assimilated by players. Anything that disrupts these functions is detrimental to the player's emotional and mental engagement with the narrative: such as loading screens, a new control scheme introduced at a critical moment, or menus and visually jarring information presented in the user interface.

Platform developers should also take note on how in-game alerts can affect storytelling. Alerts such as unlocked trophies and friend log-in notifications are a feature on most gaming platforms, including PlayStation, Xbox, and Valve's Steam platform. Such in-game alerts can pop-up inappropriately during the most delicate storytelling moments that should otherwise be reserved for player contemplation. Such visual interruptions are equivalent to a person's cell phone going off in the cinema just after Frodo manages to destroy The Ring in the lava of Mount Doom. Alerts certainly add value to gaming by rewarding players and enabling social connectivity. However, in the context of storytelling, alerts often have negative affects on the player's narrative experience. It's therefore important that developers or players wishing to focus on a story are given functions that allow them to deactivate such gaming features.

End-of-Level Menus

Certain games present players with a stat menu on completing each mission. In doing so, developers indicate that gameplay takes precedence over the story because the player is encouraged to contemplate his or her skill-based achievements—like in a sports match—not the aesthetic experience of the narrative. This approach is neither right nor wrong, but highlights the need for developers to decide upfront whether their game sits on the ludic or narrative side of game design. Developers who choose to focus on narrative must endeavor to orchestrate seamless transitions that are not interrupted by menus and scoreboards.

Dramatic Disconnect

The focus of a transition should be the unexpected turn of events that occurs at the dramatic climax. This experience should ideally be followed by a quiet moment of low activity that gives players time to contemplate the turning point and experience the transition's emotional echo (Figure 12.1). Instead, narrative-driven games occasionally forgo pacing by succeeding the transition with high-tension gameplay. The flurry of action set pieces and cutscenes that occur in the intervening time from the turning point means that players become victims of vigilance fatigue—overwhelmed with information that breaks the clarity of the transition's functional parts. The misguided thinking is that more action equals a richer story.

Film directors naturally have more flexibility when orchestrating transitions because of the absence of attention-consuming gameplay. Nonetheless, consider how adding action-packed events after the transition would affect the audience's perception of the narrative for *The Lord of the Rings: The Two Towers* (Figure SII.4) if the presumed trampling of Pippin had been followed up by a second battle scene—such as the film's finale at Helm's Deep. The action at Helm's Deep would diminish the effectiveness of the contemplative moment underscored by Legolas (Figure SII.5) due to the constant activity that overshadows Pippin's predicament.

Figure 12.1 A dramatic structure that maintains a high level of tension and gameplay results in players having no quiet time to contemplate and emotionally engage with the narrative due to attention bottleneck.

Paused Gameplay

Additionally, players who wish to pause their gameplay session will often do so immediately after the transition at the point marked with a pause icon in Figure 12.1. The transition marks a new scene, so it makes for a logical drop-off point before a new dramatic sequence begins to unfold. If the contemplative space is replaced with high-tension action, players will likely walk away with the posttransition action lingering on their minds, not the important pretransition turning point. Upon resuming gameplay, they will again be plunged into a high-tension situation. It is therefore crucial that transitions are structured correctly due to the stop–start nature of playing games, which are rarely completed in one sitting.

Delayed Turning Point

Similar narrative problems can occur if the turning point is delayed for too long—gradually lessening the anticipation of a rewarding climactic event. This happens through various factors both within and outside the design team's control: a level may be too long; obstacles may be too difficult for certain players to overcome; players may get lost in the environment; or the context of their actions is not sufficiently reiterated to remind them of what is at stake. A problematic variable is player proficiency and video game literacy, which varies widely from person to person and can only be overcome with a lot of testing during a game's development. Using the combined techniques in this book will help designers to reduce the possibilities of such situations, and help orchestrate gameplay moments that significantly enhance the story experience.

Lack of Escalating Tension

With the ever-increasing narrative scope of games, designers must find new ways to generate dramatic tension aside from action-based mechanics. Tension in games has tendentiously been orchestrated by steadily ramping-up difficulty of gameplay. Such an approach may not be appropriate when dealing with subtler subject matter. This is particularly true of gameplay segments that focus on basic progression without conflict, such as the player's activity prior to meeting GLaDOS in the *Portal 2* transition (Chapter 10, Case Study: *Portal 2* section) in which the player's progression has a purely narrative function set aside from the game's core gameplay. The designers of *Portal 2* have done a commendable job of generating tension using dynamic composition and the shape concepts that we explored in Section I. Conversely, *random encounters* (where players are sporadically ambushed by enemies when traversing the game world) that occur in most role-playing games tend to suffer from a lack of emotional engagement. This is because these battles tend to happen without foreshadowing, which means that players are not emotionally primed for a dramatic event—thus reducing random encounters to episodes of strategic gameplay without emotional empathy. Designers must therefore use varying aesthetics to generate an escalation of tension. Few get it right like *Portal 2*, which results in narrative disconnect because players are not suitably primed to anticipate a turning point and end up feeling apathetic when the dramatic event suddenly and unexpectedly occurs.

Summary

We can see that interactivity creates many complications for storytelling, which can lead to confusing or emotionally meaningless gameplay experiences due to inconsistent control schemes, misplaced menus, in-game alerts, and gameplay that does not adhere to the conventions of dramatic structure. The challenge of mitigating such issues becomes exponentially harder the bigger the game development budget and team size because this usually coincides with more ambitious games that are inherently complex and difficult to test. This is one of several reasons why a storytelling framework that encompasses the whole team is so vital. The above examples of transition hazards serve a vital purpose of reiterating the base functions of transitions and the dramatic curve, recapped below, to ensure that players experience a fulfilling narrative irrespective of the genre:

Call-to-action (before): an inciting event sets the context for ensuing action

Mounting tension (before): tension is gradually ramped-up to prime the audience to anticipate a key event in the story

Turning point (before): presents a revelation or significant turn of events

Contemplative space (after): for contemplating the turning point and the narrative as a whole

Contrasting aesthetics (before and after): used to heighten the emotional echo

Now that we have a solid understanding for the emotional significance of video game transitions and the do's and don'ts for orchestrating them, the following chapters will explore advanced transition techniques for games without cutscenes, and open-world games.

13 Transitions without Cutscenes

The games that we examined in Chapter 10 used film-style cutscenes for communicating exposition and subtext which are difficult to convey during gameplay—when players are preoccupied with their own experiences. The case studies in the following sections include transitions from games like *Journey*, *Minecraft*, and the *Grand Theft Auto* series to demonstrate how emotionally rich story experiences can be orchestrated without cutscenes using the dynamic composition framework, so that interactivity remains active throughout the transition.

Case Study: *Journey*

The story in *Journey* is communicated through a wordless sequence of impressions that invite players to form their own conclusions about the narrative. Suggestion is a considerably more effective method for storytelling than explicit disclosure of narrative because it engages the player-audience's imagination and offers multiple interpretations unique to each person. The following transition from part 4 of *Journey*—commonly referred to as "The Descent"—demonstrates how the dynamic composition framework can be adapted to pure gameplay without resorting to cutscenes for story exposition.

Developer: thatgamecompany
Video search term: "Journey The Descent"

Figure 13.1 "The Descent" gameplay segment in *Journey* (2012), by thatgame-company, is a Masterclass in storytelling that exemplifies the dramatic curve's application using the strength of the interactive medium.

Transitions as Pure Gameplay

Upon passing the great wall (Figure 13.1a) the playable character is accompanied by flying creatures as the environment opens up to a wide slope filled with rolling dunes and a view of the mysterious mountain that draws the player ever closer (Figure 13.1b). The looming mountain—visible on several occasions in the upper part of the frame during the descent—serves the role of a call-to-action, as players are implicitly encouraged to consider whether they will ever reach its peak. Freedom of movement is momentarily reduced to a simple right-to-left direction when the player enters the tunnel (Figure 13.1c). To further help players calmly contemplate the mountain, which features as a backdrop, the tunnel's design is based on simple horizontal and vertical lines. The character remains grounded during these latter stages of the transition so that it can no longer jump and glide. The comfortable ride is quickly contrasted with the appearance of angular rocks along a steep narrow, zigzagging path cast in shadow (Figure 13.1d) where the character quickly accelerates down the slope—the sensation of speed emphasized by heavy overhead arches (Figure 13.1e). The character is finally flung into the air and briefly framed with a high-angle camera that captures the mountain one last time (Figure 13.1f), before tracking the character downward in a long vertical drop. All the built-up excitement comes to a sudden stop, as the player lands at the entrance to the underground tunnels, left alone to contemplate the events that have just transpired and the ominous dark caves before them (Figure 13.1g).

Dynamic Rhythm and Melody

The soundtrack, composed by Austin Wintory, underscores the flow of events with a delicate melody dominating the start and mid sections of the descent to echo the playable characters' jumping and gliding movements Figure 13.1a–c. As tension builds toward the transition, the melody is forced into the background by a heavy, staggering drumbeat that aligns with the character's grounded movements that suggest panicked steps before it falls off the edge of the cliff (Figure 13.1d,e). The pounding drums quickly dissipate and are replaced by prolonged chords that accompany the character as it falls and lands at the entrance to the tunnel (Figure 13.1f,g). The relative silence that follows is synonymous with the accompanist's technique that we explored in Chapter 7 (Figure 7.15), where lowering the volume is used to draw in the audience that is careful not to miss anything that may be whispered in the musical vacuum.

The Core Aesthetic Mechanic

On analyzing the dynamic composition elements of *Journey*'s transition we can see that the degree of pathway incline defines the tempo of gameplay (Figure 13.2). The character's speed is concurrent with slope angle, so that players instinctively understand when a change of pace is about to occur. When the slope has a medium tilt (Figure 13.1b), the character slides down the mountain at a medium speed. When tension is to be ramped up or knocked back before and after the transition, the designers need simply increase or flatten the slope angle, respectively. The shift of slope angle is complimented by pathway shapes that

		⬤ Optimism	▲ Danger	⬛ Pessimism
	Lines of movement	Uplifting	Grounded and fast	Grounded and slow
	Environment shapes	Rolling	Angular	Flat
	Pathways	Wide or "open canvas"	Angular and steep	Flat
	Audio	Uplifting melody	Staggering rhythm	White noise
	Player gestures	Freeform	Reactive	Ponderous

Figure 13.2 The active elements of dynamic composition are expertly interwoven to reflect the buoyant and uplifting actions of the playable character as it goes from aerial glides to grounded slides.

range from wide open to narrow and angular. A narrative is automatically created in the player's mind because of the changing circumstances of the character, communicated through invigorating aerials and speed that transition to a heavy feeling when the character becomes grounded. Pathways are therefore *Journey*'s core aesthetic mechanic.

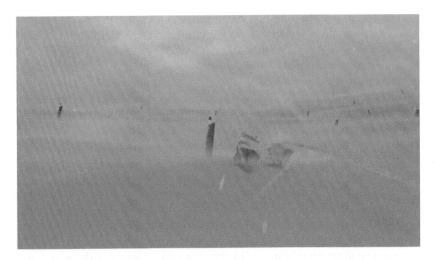

Figure 13.3 The core aesthetic mechanic is complimented by storm winds that buffet the playable character from left and right during the final ascent in *Journey* (2012), by thatgamecompany.

Note that buffeting winds that affect the lines of movement become an additional core aesthetic mechanic, alongside pathways, toward the end of *Journey* when the playable character approaches the summit and must wearily trudge uphill in the midst of a snowstorm (Figure 13.3). Traversal is made problematic as the character is pummeled from left and right—eliciting angular gestures from players as they attempt to assert a forward movement.

Narrative-Gameplay Harmony

Journey's development team made great efforts to reiterate the context of the player's actions by ensuring the mountain is framed by the in-game camera at several points during the descent (Figure 13.1b,c,f). To increase the player's ability to contemplate this important end goal, controls are simplified to a single axis during the tunnel section (Figure 13.1c), which alleviates problems of attention bottleneck by limiting the player's interactive possibilities.

The reason why narrative and gameplay are so closely interwoven along *Journey*'s dramatic curve is due to the absence of animated cutscenes (Figure 13.4). The player's interpretation of the story is derived solely from diagetic cues in the environment and the flow of gameplay. The scene transition starts off as a graceful and leisurely slide down the mountain and finishes as an energetic rollercoaster ride with a cliff drop before halting at the foot of the tunnel. The point at which players have one last view of the mountain (Figure 13.1f) signifies the dramatic turning point, which subconsciously poses the question for the player to contemplate: Will they ever reach the mountain and learn its secrets? After the transition the aesthetics are abruptly inverted by a low-tension state that creates the vital emotional echo. The high-tension aesthetics before the transition (Figure 13.1d,e) foreshadow the subsequent underground tunnel sequence where the player first encounters the threatening Guardians.

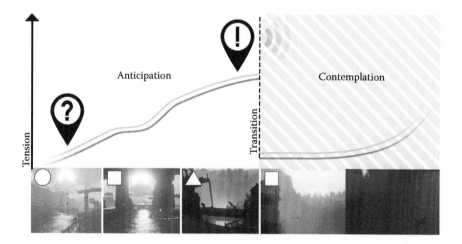

Figure 13.4 The dramatic curve reveals the perfect alignment between narrative and gameplay for *Journey*'s masterful transition.

Replay

Journey, by thatgamecompany
Publisher: Sony Computer Entertainment

thatgamecompany skillfully orchestrated this powerful transition because of the aesthetic-driven approach to game design, in which the player is instrumental to the story's progress—retaining control of the playable character throughout the transition. When tension is low the player can comfortably consider the mystery and beauty of the mountain. When tension is high, attention bottleneck reduces the player's concerns to oncoming obstacles in their immediate environment. This gameplay sequence also demonstrates best practice for the call-to-action, which is more effective if it's communicated diegetically within the game. With such an approach players must react to changing circumstances that they personally experience—rather than act on commands delivered via noninteractive cutscenes. It is recommended that you play through "The Descent" sequence in *Journey* several times to consecutively study each aspect of dynamic composition and gameplay—such as lines of movement, environment shapes, and music—to appreciate the sophisticated orchestration of this experience.

Case Study: *Gone Home*

Another game that breaks many design molds is *Gone Home* (2013), by The Fullbright Company. Our dynamic composition framework nonetheless allows us to identify an objective structure within the game's innovative approach to narrative. Please note that the following analysis includes spoilers.

Developer: The Fullbright Company
Video search term: "Gone Home Walkthrough"

Drama Analysis

From the outset *Gone Home* presents a pastiche of horror film motifs. On a dark and stormy night the player—representing a 21-year-old girl called Kaitlin—arrives on the porch of her family's house after a year of traveling to find her parents are not home and neither is her sister, Samantha (Sam). This call-to-action motivates the player to explore the vacant house searching for clues that reveal the experiences of her family during her time away. The player quickly discovers a breadcrumb trail of audio journals from Sam, which document her sister's growing affections for a girl called Lonnie. The rooms of the house are mostly unlit upon entering (Figure 13.5a), giving the player a sense of trepidation until the light switch is located in each new location (Figure 13.5b). Just when audio journals reveal that Sam's parents did not approve of her relationship with Lonnie,

Figure 13.5 *Gone Home* (2013), by The Fullbright Company, is a patchwork of narrative genres that are successfully brought together to create an immensely touching story of love and friendship.

vacant family spaces give way to service passageways and a basement featuring a nightmarish furnace (Figure 13.5d,e)—much like the one that torments Kevin McCallister, played by Macaulay Culkin, in *Home Alone* (1990). Packing boxes (Figure 13.5f) herald Lonnie's departure for army service duty, to the distress of Sam. The mood takes an ominous turn in subsequent audio journals in which Sam laments Lonnie's leaving, and the player discovers a secret room containing the attic key and a pentagram (Figure 13.5g)—references to Sam's interest in the occult that were planted earlier in the story. The attic door opens up like an anthropomorphized mouth with a contemptuous gaze (Figure 13.5h), which the player must ascend with a great sense of dread at what they might find upstairs. A powerful catharsis overcomes players when an audio journal reveals that Sam is, in fact, safe and happily reunited with her love, Lonnie (Figure 13.5i). The story finishes when the player reaches the circular room within the turret of the house, where Sam's physical journal is located (Figure 13.5j).

Minimalist Dynamic Composition

The snapshot sequence in Figure 13.6 reveals that *Gone Home* uses a very limited set of dynamic composition elements that support the narrative events communicated through dialogue. Sam's beautifully voice-acted performance by actress, Sarah Grayson, delivers an intimate series of audio journals that take players through Sam's angst-ridden relationship with Lonnie: from their first kiss; to Sam being grounded and her feelings of alienation; the heartbreaking departure of Lonnie; and the uplifting reunion that signals Sam's rightful freedom to be herself. The game's core mechanic is represented by a succession of locked doors, which serve to bookend segments of exploration. The action of activating a light switch to illuminate each room (Figure 13.5a,b) can be thought of as mini transitions that shift the game's visual aesthetic from dark to light. The attic door marks the final transition once all other rooms have been unlocked and explored. The attic door's overhead placement exudes a sense of

	■ Confined	▲ Heartbroken	● Free
Pathways	Many locked doors	Final locked door	All doors unlocked
Dialogue	Alienation	Melancholy	Togetherness
Framing	Doors at eye-level	Overhead door, top of house	Not applicable

Figure 13.6 The snapshot sequence for *Gone Home* demonstrates that it's not necessary to use every element of dynamic composition to orchestrate an emotionally meaningful transition.

overbearing menace that amplifies tension, which is abruptly overturned when players discover that the attic does not contain a horror-film ending and no jump-scares will occur. The core aesthetic mechanic can therefore be identified as the audio journals and occult motifs, which set the emotional context for the player's actions.

Narrative Misdirection

What is exceptional about *Gone Home*'s approach to storytelling is the disconnect between the scripted narrative—that of Sam's love for Lonnie—and the player's experiences during explorative gameplay. The audio journals, written memos, and occult motifs scattered throughout *Gone Home* function as communication channels for the game's unreliable gamemaster (a concept that we explored in Chapter 9, The Unreliable Gamemaster section) that misdirect players into forming inexact conclusions about their role within the game. If Sam's audio journals were removed and the game featured only environmental sound effects of thunder and rain, *Gone Home* would clearly fall into the suspense-horror genre that takes place in a "Psycho house"—despite its lack of monsters and murderous figures. If, on the other hand, the audio journals were heard independent of the game—without any supporting visuals or gameplay—the audience would experience a touching romance filled with a mix of elation, teenage angst, and social issues. The magic of *Gone Home* is that it combines these two genres—suspense-horror and teenage romance—so that players empathize with the protagonist even though the objects of their fears are not the same: players fear for their own safety during their lonely wanderings and the protagonist fears the loss of their loved one. As a result, most players incorrectly assume that the objective of gameplay is to find the dead bodies of Sam and Lonnie, which they reason through the following deduction:

Distressing Audio Journals + Occult and Horror Motifs = Suicide

This is why the dramatic curve for *Gone Home* has been adapted to include positive and negative tension, so as to emphasize the implied horror aspect of the game's setting (Figure 13.7). This is the core strength of the unreliable gamemaster, who uses conventional mechanics to drive gameplay but subverts the game's victory conditions for emotional effect.

In essence, the old Victorian house that forms the setting for the game represents the nebulous mind of Sam (Figure 13.8). The closed doors (highlighted in purple on the map) symbolize obstacles in Sam's life. Each newly opened door reveals another facet of Sam's experiences until there is only one space left unexplored: the attic. Player's experience catharsis once they ascend the attic staircase bathed in blood-red light to learn that the two girls are safe, and there is no horror movie ending awaiting them. Thus, *Gone Home* successfully enables the player-audience to experience the joys and fears of Sam, even if they're not a teenage girl experiencing discrimination for her sexuality, and an uncertain future with the person she loves. The game notably achieves a high level of drama without resorting to physical conflict.

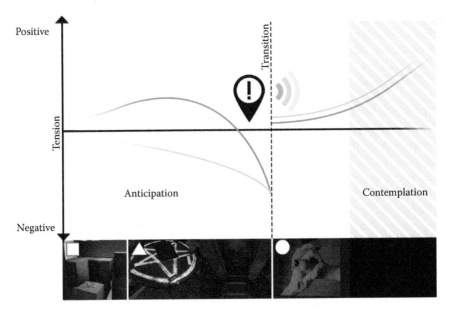

Figure 13.7 *Gone Home*'s dramatic curve uses a scale of positive and negative tension to illustrate how the differing dramatic motivations between narrative and gameplay come together at the game's cathartic turning point.

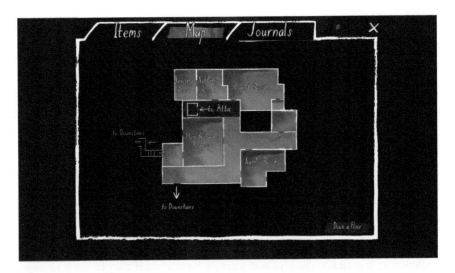

Figure 13.8 The Victorian house in which *Gone Home* (2013), by Fullbright, takes place represents the protagonist's mind—each door the player unlocks leading to a new discovery about Sam's troubled teenage existence.

Summary

Journey and *Gone Home* demonstrate how all the elements of a game can work hand in hand to create sophisticated narrative experiences unique to the medium of video games without the need for cinematic cutscenes. The ideal is that video games dispense with cutscenes altogether to create a purer form of in-game storytelling that embraces the medium's strengths. This does not necessarily mean that games without cutscenes must deliver a constant stream of activity. Equally rewarding are moments of respite so that players can reflect on their situation or contemplate the next gameplay move.

A concept introduced in Chapter 8, Calibration and Synchronization, highlighted that games like *Journey*—which carefully modulate the playable character's range of movements to fit the narrative—have a higher chance of aligning the player's experience with the game's playable character. For instance, when *Journey*'s narrative implies a relaxed and carefree environment, the character can jump and glide gracefully. When the situation turns treacherous, the character becomes grounded and slower—thus aligning the player's gestures to match the aesthetics of the narrative. In contrast, games that allow a full aesthetic range of movements—irrespective of narrative conditions—run a higher risk of players using gestures that are discordant with the game's narrative.

A characteristic common to all the games that we've explored in Section II, thus far, is *linear gameplay*. Linear gameplay is a term used to describe games that employ restricted paths to control the action and ensure that players consistently experience the sequence of events purposely designed by the game's narrative designers (also see Chapter 5, Branching Narratives section). This approach does not necessarily result in a mundane experience because a cunning mix of puzzles, dynamic gameplay situations, and minor branching routes can mask the fact that the player's progression is being channeled along a predefined course. Linear gameplay makes it easier to adapt storytelling techniques from the linear medium of film. But what happens when gameplay is set in an open world, where players can determine their own narrative pathways? The following chapter explores how the dynamic composition framework can help developers manage the incredibly complex task of storytelling in open-world games like *Minecraft* and the *Grand Theft Auto* series.

(14) Transitions in Open-World Games

Games that we've explored in the preceding chapters feature gameplay set in environments that are mostly experienced linearly, which means that every player will encounter a prescribed sequence of events in more-or-less the same order. In contrast, the genre of open-world games like *Minecraft*, and the *Grand Theft Auto* series gives players near-infinite freedom to explore sprawling 3D environments at their own will. Such games significantly reduce the game designer's ability to predict player activity because the sandbox nature of such environments means that player's can set personal gameplay challenges and enact their own stories. This raises the question of whether designers of open-world games can incorporate the dramatic curve and transition techniques without depriving players of their freedom. The critical issue is tracking the player's self-instigated call-to-action and turning points since players are free to set their own challenges. In the following case studies, we will explore various possibilities to apply our dynamic composition framework to open-world games, irrespective of this ambiguity and reduced design foresight.

Case Study: *Minecraft*

Minecraft—the brainchild of indie developer, Markus "Notch" Persson—is arguably the most successful game of all time. What draws the 22 million plus players to inhabit *Minecraft*'s procedurally generated world is the seemingly limitless possibilities for player-driven stories that involve the game's multipurpose blocks as resources or architectural tools. Despite player freedom, the game has an elegantly simple method to orchestrate dramatic transitions that has similar effects to those that we've explored in linear games.

Developer: Mojang
Video search term: "Minecraft Survive Your First Night"

An attempt to map the primary shape concepts—the circle, square, and triangle—to a game that has a singular cube aesthetic may seem absurd. However, the phenomenally successful *Minecraft* does feature aesthetic variation derived from the game's day-night cycle and the increased threat level that comes with nightfall, when the landscape fills with hostiles like the iconic Creepers and Zombies (Figure 14.1)—as we explored in Chapter 5, Character Classes section.

The rectangular sun sets every 20 minutes—an event for which players must prepare by building and maintaining shelters to fend off the ensuing onset of enemies. Safety and calm is restored once the rectangular sun rises in the morning and the player is once again free to explore the landscape and mine resources in preparation for the following night when the anxious lookout for enemies resumes. The ebb and flow of safety versus danger that comes with *Minecraft*'s day-night cycle is the game's core aesthetic mechanic—shaping player activity, gestures, and nonverbal dialogue between characters (Figure 14.2).

The day-night/safety-danger cycle creates an organic dramatic curve that is *pervasive*—affecting players irrespective of their location within the game world (Figure 14.3). Imagine how the game would play without the tension-building sunset, and dangerous creatures that come at night. The impetus to plan ahead and organize activity around *Minecraft*'s circadian rhythm would be removed and replaced by ambient monotony. The day-night cycle therefore gives context

Figure 14.1 The 20-minute day-night cycles of *Minecraft* (2011), by Mojang, drive the game's dramatic tension, guiding players toward playful activity in the daytime and survival gameplay at night.

	⬤ Freedom	◼ Defence	▲ Danger
⛰ Environment shapes	Safety and exploration	Building of shelter	Enemy characters
💬 Dialogue	Friendly	Neutral	Agitated or aggressive
🔄 Player gestures	Casual	Purposeful	Agitated or aggressive

(Transition marked before the Danger column)

Figure 14.2 *Minecraft*'s snapshot sequence reveals the fundamental role that secondary characters have in shaping the dramatic experience of the game—eliciting varying types of nonverbal dialogue depending on the time of day.

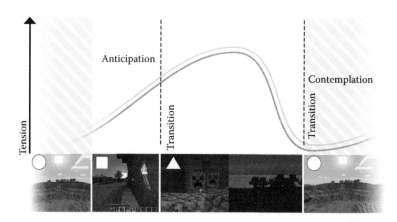

Figure 14.3 *Minecraft*'s hostile enemies begin to appear at sunset, which is an event that organically drives gameplay toward survival activities irrespective of where players find themselves in the environment.

and pacing to *Minecraft*, and the game's freeform nature means that each cycle is different depending on the player's current activities and their location within the procedurally generated world. Players are therefore more likely to equip their character with a mining axe by day and a protective sword by night. The transition is perhaps not as dramatic as previous case studies because the gradual change from night to day does not feature an abrupt cut that heightens aesthetic contrast. For an example that combines *Minecraft*'s open-world dramatic curve with a sudden change in aesthetics we can look to the *Grand Theft Auto* series and the series' "rampage mode" gameplay.

Case Study: *Grand Theft Auto*

A similar dramatic mechanism to *Minecraft*'s can be found in the *Grand Theft Auto (GTA)* series, which offers players both scripted and player-driven stories. We explored the concept of scripted storytelling in Chapter 5 on Dialogue. Scripted stories are exemplified in the gameplay of *The Last of Us: Left Behind*, and *Portal 2*, in which the narrative designers predefine a story that can be replayed as many times as the player wishes.

Developer: Rockstar North
Video search term: "GTA 5 Police Chase"

The counterpart to scripted stories in *GTA V* (2013) are story missions that players can choose to undertake at their own pace. Exposition for scripted stories happens predominantly through cutscenes and cell phone calls from accomplices, which direct players to predetermined locations in the open-world environment that serve as story checkpoints.

The second category of storytelling that coexists in *GTA*'s open world takes the form of player-driven stories. We've already explored player-driven stories in the sandbox gameplay of *Minecraft*, which affords players the freedom to shape their own activities. An instance of player-driven stories in *GTA V* happens when players decide to go on a "rampage"—an inciting event that usually begins with the player shooting an innocent bystander and ends with a high-octane chase as the player fends off gunfire from police, SWAT teams, and the FBI (Figure 14.4). The player's rampage rating—visualized as stars in the top right-hand corner of the frame—grows correspondingly to the escalating carnage. As tension rises, the key question in the player's mind is whether she will successfully evade capture, get "wasted" (injured) or "busted" (arrested). Irrespective of which outcome the player experiences, the result is that the player's wanted meter is reset to zero, the police chase is called-off, and the city returns to its default pedestrian pace. The soundscape of violence preceding the climatic turning point is correspondingly extinguished—thus creating a moment of quiet contemplation in the dramatic aftermath.

Replay

Grand Theft Auto V (2013), by Rockstar
Publisher: Rockstar Games
Load-up *GTA V* or any title in the series and initiate rampage mode. Similar to the rogue agents flag (Figure 5.7) in Ubisoft's *The Division*, which we explored in Chapter 5, notice how *GTA*'s system also moderates your behavior the more chaos you cause. Can you manage to reduce your police wanted rating back to zero once you've initiated rampage mode? Can you also discern the emotional echo after rampage mode is resolved?

Figure 14.4 Players of *Grand Theft Auto V* (2013), by Rockstar Games, can personally initiate a dramatic curve whenever they break the law—such as by shooting an innocent nonplayable character—which activates their police wanted rating.

GTA's core game mechanic involves shooting, melee fighting, and driving. The core aesthetic mechanics are predictably environment shapes that consist primarily of AI-controlled members of the public, police, and vehicles. The snapshot sequence in Figure 14.5 highlights the key elements of dynamic composition that serve to orchestrate tension build-up once a player commits to a shooting spree and rampage mode is initiated. At this stage the everyday activity and hubbub of Los Santos and its virtual citizens turns into a backdrop for a large-scale police chase—with the player at the dramatic epicenter—to the audio accompaniment of explosions, police sirens, and screeching tires. Players can actively choose to provoke more havoc or reduce tension with law-abiding behavior.

As per the dynamic composition framework, the tension-building shape concepts are countered after the transition—creating an emotional echo by contrasting the moment of highest tension with the tranquility after the chase is resolved. At this stage the players can relax, put down the controller if they wish, and contemplate the exciting events that just transpired.

The significance of this storytelling system is that it works autonomously to balance player-driven activity in the game's open world. The player retains control of when and where the call-to-action is to occur, while the game's narrative designers have embedded mechanisms that monitor tension—visualized in the form of the player's rampage rating that increases relative to their criminal activity (Figure 14.6). Although *GTA*'s depictions of violence are not to everyone's

		● Free-roaming	▲ Rampage	■ Reset
☺	Character shapes and poses	Neutral	Assault pose, or damaged vehicle	Upright
➤●	Lines of movement	Casual walking or driving	Running and firing, or speeding	Stationary
▲▲	Environment shapes	Neutral NPCs	Enemy NPCs and vehicles	No NPCs
💬	Dialogue	Playful	Violent	Alone
♪	Audio	Ambient city noise	Police sirens, destruction and gunfire	Quiet
↻	Player gestures	Casual	Aggressive	Restful

(Transition marked between Rampage and Reset columns)

Figure 14.5 The snapshot sequence for *GTA V*'s rampage mode illustrates a circle-triangle-square sequence of shape concepts that modulate the aesthetic value of active dynamic composition elements across the transition.

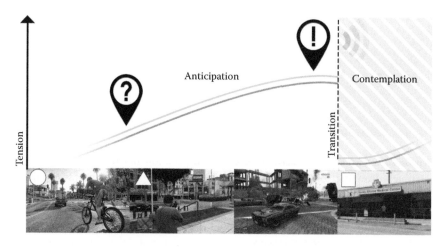

Figure 14.6 The dramatic curve for *GTA V*'s rampage mode highlights the harmony between narrative and gameplay—largely because the player is responsible for instigating and provoking dramatic tension.

tastes, the game's design has important applications for all manner of open-world games in which a dramatic curve is desired to make player activity more memorable and emotionally impactful. In practice, this means programmatically incorporating the concept of a snapshot sequence into background systems, so that high-tension gameplay mechanics can be tracked without restricting the player's possibilities to experience their own player-driven stories. The following case study proposes another advanced method for realizing dramatic structure in open-world games while accounting for player freedom.

Case Study: *Left 4 Dead*

Valve Corporation's *Left 4 Dead* series—developed in collaboration with Turtle Rock Studios—is not an open-world game per se, but nonetheless has the most far-reaching potential for the future of storytelling in this, and many other genres.

Developer: Valve Corporation, and Turtle Rock Studios
Video search term: "Left 4 Dead Walkthrough"

The series features a system called the "AI Director," which actively monitors and dynamically influences dramatic events in the game—much like a film director. The three phases of its functionality mirror our dynamic composition framework, including: a build up, peak-phase, turning point, and a period of recuperation and contemplation.

Left 4 Dead's four-player cooperative gameplay begins with a dramatic build up that gradually escalates tension by loading a small number of wandering zombies (Figure 14.7). Tension continues to ramp-up with the appearance of larger mobs and special enemies while each player's skill and stress levels are being monitored. Stress is calculated by the duration that players are under attack, the

Figure 14.7 *Left 4 Dead 2* (2012), by Valve Corporation and Turtle Rock Studios, generates dramatic tension programmatically—starting with a build-up phase that introduces a small number of zombies.

number of zombies they encounter, whether the player is injured, and the proximity of attacks. Melee combat is recognized as more stressful than long-range combat. Because stress levels are monitored per player, the AI Director can crank up or tone down the action for individuals. If players stay in one location for too long, the AI Director will increase enemy levels to motivate players to move forward.

At peak phases, the AI Director loads the largest number of regular, special, and boss enemies like the Tank and Witch (Figure 14.8). The system can also dynamically adjust pathways to hinder player progress, and audio to help generate a cinematic sense of anticipation just prior to a change in action. The most memorable gameplay moments naturally occur during the turning point, when players experience highs of victory or lows of defeat. The AI Director ensures that peak intensity varies across the game—reaching its highest level of intensity at the end of each map in time for a fitting finale.

Figure 14.8 The peak phase in *Left 4 Dead 2* (2012), by Valve Corporation and Turtle Rock Studios, sees players defending against the toughest and largest number of enemies.

Figure 14.9 As with all earlier examples of transitions in video games, the moment after the turning point in *Left 4 Dead 2* (2012), by Valve Corporation and Turtle Rock Studios, also features a moment of contemplation when players can recuperate and exchange war stories.

The recuperation phase simultaneously serves as the moment of contemplation for prior events, allowing the 4-player team to share their war stories (Figure 14.9). During this phase, the AI Director loads in additional health packs and ammunition so that players can top-up health, and reload weapons before the whole cycle repeats.

The concept of AI-driven storytelling is currently limited to a few games. However, such a procedural approach to storytelling is a highly effective solution for directing player-driven stories in open-world games where player activity cannot always be predicted by development teams. The dynamic composition framework—composed of primary shapes, dynamic composition, and the dramatic curve—that we've explored throughout this book makes for a perfect basis upon which to develop such mechanisms that place precedence on the aesthetic experience of gameplay. In the words of Gabe Newell, managing director of Valve Corporation:

> One of the theories of fun we use is that the more ways in which the game is recognizing and responding to player choices, the more fun it seems.

Summary

Despite their free-form nature, the games featured in this chapter demonstrate that open-world games can be designed to deliver the same dramatic structure that we find in scripted narratives. The key concept is to monitor player activity for tension—adjusting in-game events to fit the dramatic curve on the fly (*The Division*, the *GTA* series, and *Left 4 Dead*). Alternatively, games can feature gameplay that continually undulates between low and high tension, driven by the behavior of secondary characters or environmental conditions (*Minecraft*). The diminished ability to foresee player intentions in open-world environments is compensated by a reduced need to reiterate gameplay objectives (see Chapter 11, Reiteration of Themes and Gameplay Objectives), since each player will have his or her self-appointed goals clearly in mind.

This concludes our exploration of storytelling in video games. The case studies that we have examined demonstrate how traditional storytelling techniques can be applied to all manner of gameplay types—from linear to open-world games, and games with and without cutscenes.

Conclusion

Gaming's often misguided tendency is to lead design by a genre or style and use escalating difficulty and aggression to create dramatic tension. Dramatic tension isn't concordant with difficulty, as we've seen from the examples in this book. Tension can come in many forms including positive anticipation, vulnerability, or loneliness. Antagonists can also be threatening without being overly aggressive. This understanding is the key to widening the aesthetic scope of video games and the medium's ability to explore genres that celebrate diversity of gender, cultures, sexuality, ethnicity, and disability. Games are a powerful artistic tool that motivates activity and can accommodate every artistic theme. Irrespective of whether you're on the development, academic, or consumer side of the video gaming industry, the framework presented in this book will help you be more fluent in the art of interactive storytelling, and set higher standards for what constitutes a good narrative-driven video game. The untapped potential to adapt stories from films, music, paintings, and literature according to video gaming's true strengths is very exciting for the future of the medium.

Dynamic Composition Framework

It is clear from our analysis of primary shapes, dynamic composition, and the dramatic curve that embracing a dynamic approach to game aesthetics leads to heightened emotional experiences. The shape spectrum and primary shapes—so revered by the ancient Greek's for their basis in nature—provide us with a framework for comparative analysis and modulating the aesthetics of design elements to fit the needs of a narrative (Figure C.1). Ultimately, it's not the shapes that are important, but the emotional themes that each is associated with:

Circle: innocence, youth, energy, movement, positivity, freedom, relaxation
Square: maturity, balance, stubbornness, strength, rest, restraint, rational, conservative, calm
Triangle: aggression, force, instability, pain, sorrow, tension

Figure C.1 The shape spectrum is used as a comparative analysis tool to assess the aesthetic alignment of design elements against the three primary shapes—the circle, square, and triangle—and their corresponding emotional themes.

Leading with Player Gestures

Above all, primary shapes teach us shape sensitivity, which is central to making sense of the complex visual, interactive, and audio systems of video games. For this purpose, we explored the eight elements of dynamic composition that represent our framework: character shapes and poses, lines of movement, environment shapes, pathways, dialogue, framing, audio, and player gestures. The main goal is

		Theme1	Theme2	Theme3
😀	Character shapes and poses	Description	Description	Description
	Lines of movement			
	Environment shapes			
	Pathways			
	Dialogue			
	Framing			
	Audio			
	Player gestures			

Figure C.2 A snapshot sequence table, featuring the eight elements of dynamic composition in the left column; a 3-point sequence of primary shape concepts and their respective themes in the top row; and a transition line that marks the division between adjoining gameplay segments.

to define the player's gestures to be elicited and shape the activity that they will be *doing* in the context of the narrative. Starting the design or analysis process by considering a desired set of player gestures ensures that the elements of dynamic composition that play out on-screen are designed to support the physical and emotional experiences of players (Figure C.2).

Sequences of Gameplay Vignettes

The trend toward gameplay that takes full advantage of dynamic composition concepts is exemplified in the pioneering game, *...But That Was [Yesterday]* (2010) by indie developer Michael Molinari, *The Beginner's Guide* by Everything Unlimited Ltd. (briefly explored in Chapter 3, Environment Shapes), and *That Dragon, Cancer* (2016) by Numinous Games. The latter, for instance, is an autobiographical game about a couple's real-life experiences caring for their child who was diagnosed with terminal cancer. Rather than present players with a single gameplay mechanic applied consistently throughout the game, *That Dragon, Cancer* is composed of a sequence of gameplay vignettes that explore various facets of dealing with death. Fleeting moments of happiness, triumph, and optimism (Figure C.3a) are contrasted with moments of sorrow and withdrawal (Figure C.3b) using gameplay mechanics to convey each aesthetic. The final outcome is an emotionally complex experience that would not have been possible if the game's designers had focussed on a single core gameplay mechanic—an approach typical to most games.

Snapshot Sequences and the Dramatic Curve

Dynamic composition enabled us to take objective snapshots of a video game's overall design at key moments of a story. These key moments were applied to the dramatic curve that requires a minimum of three aesthetic phases to create a transition curve—without which we would have monotony. Note that the dramatic curve can also be used to structure the overarching narrative, with each gameplay sequence contributing to a satisfying build up in tension toward a climactic ending (Figure C.4).

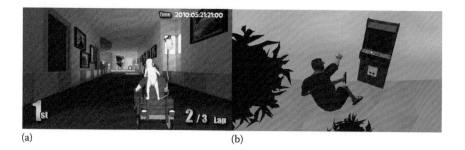

(a)   (b)

Figure C.3 *That Dragon, Cancer* (2016), by Numinous Games, presents players with a sequence of varied gameplay vignettes that explore several facets of dealing with the death of a loved one—from moments of optimism and joy (a) to withdrawal and sorrow (b).

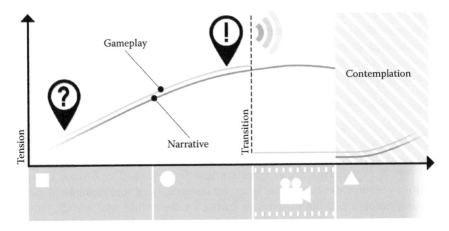

Figure C.4 The dramatic curve adapted for video game design, which introduces a gameplay thread alongside narrative, but otherwise has the same structure as for traditional storytelling.

The call-to-action is what motivates the player to engage with the narrative. This can be as subtle as presenting players with a mysterious landscape or landmark (Figure 11.10, *Dear Esther*), an intriguing situation (Chapter 13, Case Study: *Gone Home* section), or the threat of encroaching enemies (Chapter 14, Case Study: *Minecraft* section). The call-to-action represents the context that motivates players to pick up the game controller and act. However, we should always remember that in real life we rarely welcome life-changing events with such a carefree attitude as when playing video games. This occurs because players have much less to lose in the make-believe worlds of video games and the reason why lasting consequences for player actions are an important ingredient for dramatic tension. Games like *Life Is Strange* and *Resident Evil 2* demonstrate that the best method to induce hesitation is to engage the player's imagination in visualizing the consequences that may or may not be true (Chapter 9, The Call-to-Action and Refusal of the Call section). Frédérick Raynal, designer of *Alone in the Dark* (1992), summarized it perfectly when he said: "Imagination is stronger than polygons." And this, of course, also applies to gameplay objectives that—as in *Gone Home*—are never explicitly communicated to players. Instead, players must interpret their purpose in the game from incomplete information deliberately planted by the unreliable gamemaster (Chapter 9, The Unreliable Gamemaster section).

Contrast and Clarity

Contrast is a vital secondary theme of this book—alongside primary shapes—for emphasizing an idea or emotion. Aesthetic contrasts are used variably, such as for amplifying emotions, directing the player's gaze, and infusing characters with more depth. To understand the importance of contrast, consider the visual impression of an open flame in broad daylight versus nighttime. In daylight the flame is barely perceptible while at night it becomes a powerful visual focal point that demands attention. Contrast across a storytelling transition is used in this way to heighten the player-audience's ability to think about and feel the narrative. The essence of any story should likewise be presented against a contrasting backdrop if it is to make an equally powerful impression on the player-audience.

Interactive Story Checklist

The following checklist provides points to help sharpen your assessment of interactive stories:

- What is the call-to-action that sets the context for ensuing action?
- What is the turning point that is presented at the peak of dramatic tension?
- What is the core game mechanic that defines the player's primary abilities?
- What is the core aesthetic mechanic, which has the greatest influence to modulate the emotional experience of the core game mechanic?
- Can each element of the game be modulated to elicit three distinct aesthetics?
- Are players suitably primed to anticipate an important turning point at the dramatic climax of a transition?
- Is there an appropriate period of contemplation following a transition, during which the player can conceivably put down the controller without consequence?
- Do the aesthetics before and after the transition sufficiently contrast each other to heighten the emotional echo and make the turning point more resonant?
- Is every active element of dynamic composition vital to the story, or could some be removed for simplification and clarity?
- Does the player's set of gestures reflect the actions of his or her on-screen character?
- Could the control scheme be simplified to increase player immersion?

Subverting Expectations

The dynamic composition framework presented in this book is deliberately flexible to accommodate the multidisciplined nature of video games. It is therefore arguably the most inclusive design language that we can hope for. Nonetheless, using intuition and going against convention is certainly more desirable. Consider the depth of character that we perceive in a wild shark and its graceful meanderings, which belie its ferocious capabilities. Equally, a video game character that is villainous in appearance, but turns out to be a hero, will surprise players and make their experience emotionally richer and more engaging. Irrespective of a game's story choices, the entire team's fluency in shape concepts and dynamic composition is the key. Christopher Vogler— author of *The Writer's Journey: Mythic Structure for Writers* (Sheridan Books Inc., 1998)—gives the following advice, which we can apply to our design process:

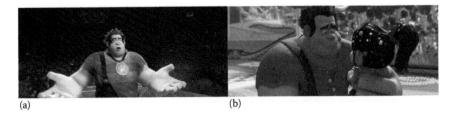

(a)   (b)

Figure C.5 The *want* of Wreck-It Ralph—the protagonist in the film (2012) of the same name by Walt Disney Animation Studios—is to win a hero's medal (a) but his spiritual *need* is to become a noble person by accepting his own quirks and caring for others (b).

> If you get lost, refer to the metaphor as you would check a map on a journey. But don't mistake the map for the journey. You don't drive with a map pasted to your windshield. You consult it before setting out or when you get disorientated. The joy of a journey is not reading or following a map, but exploring unknown places and wandering off the map now and then. It's only by getting creatively lost, beyond the boundaries of tradition, that new discoveries can be made.

In fact, rather than constrain creativity, developing sensitivity for shape concepts will improve creativity! This is because creativity is nothing more than *the ability to make abstract connections between seemingly disparate things.* The universality of the circle, square, and triangle shape concepts highlights just how interconnected everything is—enabling us to make abstract connections that may have otherwise been overlooked.

The Heart of the Story

The artistic scope of video games will continue to grow as we increasingly take inspiration from diverse sources. At the center of every great story—irrespective of the medium—is a theme of spiritual transformation. Iain McCaig emphasises that it's not the protagonist's materialistic desires (their *wants*) that drive the narrative. It is their emotional *needs* that we empathize with. Wreck-It Ralph *wants* a medal to become a hero but his spiritual *need* is to become selfless and accept his personal quirks—a transformation that transpires through the lessons that he learns en route toward his false objective (Figure C.5). The real reward is therefore the journey itself, and not the perceived goal.

The premise behind a narrative-driven game should therefore begin with the question: what is the player's *emotional journey*, and how can it be conveyed through *physical gestures* (the essence of gaming's art form)?

You are warmly invited to share your ideas and application of this book's concepts using the hashtag #dynamiccomp, so that we may build a stronger interactive storytelling knowledge base for the art form.

Website: www.solarskistudio.com
Facebook: SolarskiStudio
Twitter: @SolarskiStudio

Further Reference

Selected Bibliography

Between the Scenes: What Every Film Director, Writer, and Editor Should Know about Scene Transitions (Michael Wiese Productions 2014), by Jeffrey Michael Bays.

Bloodborne Lore (Bloodborne Wiki 2015), http://bloodborne.wiki.fextralife.com /Lore.

Classical Drawing Atelier: A Contemporary Guide to Traditional Studio Practice (Watson-Guptill 2006), by Juliette Aristides.

Classical Painting Atelier: A Contemporary Guide to Traditional Studio Practice (Watson-Guptill 2008), by Juliette Aristides.

Drawing Basics and Video Game Art: Classic to Cutting-Edge Art Techniques for Winning Video Game Design (Watson-Guptill 2012), by Chris Solarski.

Emotions Revealed: Understanding Faces and Feelings (Weidenfeld & Nicholson 2003), by Paul Ekman.

Force: Dynamic Life Drawing for Animators (Focal Press 2006), by Mike Mattesi.

Framed Ink: Drawing and Composition for Visual Storytellers (Design Studio Press 2010), by Marcos Mateu-Mestre.

Game Feel: The Secret Ingredient (Gamasutra 2007), by Steve Swink, http://www .gamasutra.com/view/feature/130734/game_feel_the_secret_ingredient .php?print=1.

Game Feel: A Game Designer's Guide to Virtual Sensation (CRC Press 2009), by Steve Swink.

Hellboy Library Edition Volume 1: Seed of Destruction and Wake the Devil (Dark Horse 2008), by Mike Mignola and John Byrne.

Hero with a Thousand Faces (Pantheon Books 1949), by Joseph Campbell.

Improving Your Storytelling: Beyond the Basics for All Who Tell Stories in Work or Play (August House 1999), by Doug Lipman.

Into The Woods: How Stories Work and Why We Tell Them (Penguin 2014), by John Yorke.

In The Blink of An Eye: A Perspective on Film Editing (Silman-James Press 2001), by Walter Murch.

In the Directors Chair (2014), by Tommy Thompson, http://t2thompson.com /2014/12/01/in-the-directors-chair-left-4-dead/.

Level Design: Concept, Theory, and Practice (A K Peters 2010), by Rudolf Kremers.

Master Class in Figure Drawing (Watson-Guptill 1991), by Robert Beverly Hale.

Music Choices: Subverting Expectations (David Canela 2014), by David Canela, http://www.david-canela.com/2014/11/25/music-choices-subverting -expectations.

Picture This: How Pictures Work (SeaStar Books 2001), by Molly Bang.

Point and Line to Plane (Dover Publications, Inc. 1979), by Wassily Kandinsky.

Shadowline: The Art of Iain McCaig (Insight Editions 2008), by Iain McCaig.

Sketchbook: Composition Studies for Film (Laurence King Publishing 2015), by Hans Bacher.

Soothe Your Soul with 'Panoramical,' A Game of Musical Manipulation (Engadget 2015), by Jessica Conditt, http://www.engadget.com/2015/09/18/panoramical -finji-polytron-indie-fund/.

Sunny (Viz LLC 2013), by Taiyo Matsumoto.

The Art of Color and Design (McGraw-Hill Book Company, Inc. 1951), by Maitland Graves.

The Art of Game Design: A Book of Lenses (CRC Press 2008), by Jesse Schell.

The Art of Journey (Bluecanvas 2012), by Matt Nava.

The Elements of Drawing (J. M. Dent & Sons Ltd. 1907), by John Ruskin.

The Filmmaker's Eye: Learning (and Breaking) the Rules of Cinematic Composition (Focal Press 2010), by Gustavo Mercado.

The Illusion of Life: Disney Animation (Disney Editions 1995), by Frank Thomas and Ollie Johnston.

The Image of the City (MIT Press 1960), by Kevin Lynch.

The Music of the Silent Films (Music Sales Ltd. 2015), by Ben Model.

The Writer's Journey: Mythic Structure for Writers (Michael Wiese Productions 1998), Christopher Vogler.

Throwing Money at the Screen (Kill Screen 2016), by Justin Keever, https:// killscreen.com/articles/throwing-money-screen/.

To the Actor: On the Technique of Acting (Harper & Row, New York 1953), by Michael Chechov.

Understanding Comics: The Invisible Art (William Morrow Paperbacks 1994), by Scott McCloud.

Videos

50 Camera Mistakes (2015) by John Nesky—www.gdcvault.com.

AAA Level Design in a Day Bootcamp: Techniques for In-Level Storytelling/ Techniques for In-Level Storytelling (2013), by Steve Gaynor—www .gdcvault.com.

Art Direction Bootcamp: Cinematography for Art Directors (2015), by Robh Ruppel—www.gdcvault.com.

Attention, Not Immersion: Making Your Games Better with Psychology and Play-testing, the Uncharted Way (2012), by Richard Lemarchand—www.gdcvault.com.

Emotional Journey: BioWare's Methods to Bring Narrative into Levels (2013), by Dave Feltham—www.gdcvault.com.

Reimagining Story Structure: Moving Beyond Three-Acts in Narrative Design (2013), by Jeremy Bernstein—www.gdcvault.com.

The Level Design of Gone Home (2015), by Kate Craig and Steve Gaynor—www.gdcvault.com.

Visual Storytelling with Iain McCaig Vol. 1: Anatomy of a Story (Gnomon Workshop 2005), by Iain McCaig.

Index

Printed and bound by CPI Group (UK) Ltd, Croydon, CR0 4YY

23/10/2024

01777696-0013